INDEPENDENT ILS LIVING SCALES ™

MANUAL

Patricia Anderten Loeb

PEARSON

License to Use

You understand that You have purchased a nonexclusive, nontransferable, revocable, limited License to use the Copyrighted Material pursuant to this limited License. The purchase of this limited License in no way transfers copyrights or other ownership interests to You. You agree that You will not (and shall not permit others to) sublicense, rent, lend, transfer, lease, sell, or provide to others the Copyrighted Material. Permission is hereby granted to You to share or lend the Copyrighted Material only with another professional who meets the Publisher's qualifications for License purchase, as long as such loan or sharing does not otherwise violate this limited license.

Published by Pearson
P.O. Box 599700
San Antonio, TX 78259
800.211.8378

www.PsychCorp.com

Acknowledgments

Throughout the years I have been fortunate in knowing many intelligent, energetic, and wise older adults. As a graduate student I found that the literature on adult development and aging did not coincide with my experience of older adults; my experience was one not of progressive decline in energy and intelligence among older adults but of persistence in learning, adapting, and compensating.

While pondering this issue, I attended a lecture on law and psychology by Bruce Dennis Sales, JD, PhD. The lecture stimulated me to think about the interaction of psychology and law, and more specifically about the psychology of aging and guardianship laws. The *Independent Living Scales* (ILS) was born out of the research for my master's thesis and my doctoral dissertation at St. Louis University. I am most indebted to J. Thomas Grisso, PhD, for the mentorship he provided as Chair for my thesis and dissertation. I am also appreciative of the input from Paul Handal, PhD, and Joan M. Oliver, PhD, dissertation committee members.

I collected the initial data on the ILS (then called the *Community Competence Scale*) as a psychology intern at the College of Medicine and Dentistry of New Jersey. I am grateful to Meyer Rothberg, PhD, for his support during this internship. Following the internship, I worked with many older adults as an employee of the New York City Health and Hospitals Corporation at Goldwater Memorial. I wish to thank Herbert Zaresky, PhD, Frima Christopher, PhD, and Christopher MacDonald, PhD, for their support and input on the progressive development of the ILS. H. Russell Searight, PhD, was instrumental in conducting research on the ILS with adults with a psychiatric diagnosis, advancing the use of the ILS in that direction.

Many people at The Psychological Corporation have made significant contributions to the final edition of the ILS. Thanks go to Kathleen Matula, PhD, for working on the development of this project through standardization and for bringing it to publication. As Project Director, Dr. Matula has made a major contribution toward ensuring psychometric soundness and clinical utility of the instrument. Michelle Brummett, Research Assistant, played a key role in ensuring scoring accuracy and in enhancing the features of the ILS for adaptation with certain populations. She provided much insight after spending many hours of testing with the standardization edition. Diane Stewart and Debbie Salinas are thanked for the effort involved in overseeing and managing the data collection. Yi Mei Zia, PhD, and Hei-Ning Helen Chan are to be praised for their tireless assistance in providing technical support for the analyses as well as conducting the analyses.

Among the senior staff members of The Psychological Corporation, I wish to acknowledge Aurelio Prifitera, PhD, Vice President and Director of the Psychological Measurement Group, for helping to bring this product on board. Joanne Lenke, PhD, Executive Vice President, saw the dire need for an instrument such as the ILS and strongly supported its publication. The important support of John R. Dilworth, President of The Psychological Corporation, is also recognized.

For much work during the final stages of the *Independent Living Scales*, thanks go to Terri C. Traeger, Supervising Editor; Barbara S. Henderson, Editor; and Don Albert, Designer. The efforts of Neil Kinch, Production Manager, and of the staff of the Electronic Publishing Center are much appreciated also.

I especially want to thank my family for their important direct and indirect contributions. My parents, Pat and George Anderten; my parents-in-law, Betty and Robert Loeb; my cousin Magistrate Joan Azrack; and my husband, Thomas Loeb, MD, have been very supportive.

I would like to mention with gratitude all the examiners who extended themselves to find cases and to collect the data for the ILS standardization. I also want to thank all of the anonymous examinees who agreed to be tested with the ILS.

Patricia Loeb
Old Westbury, NY
April 1996

Table of Contents

Figures

Tables

▲ Chapter 1

Introduction

Nature and Purpose

The *Independent Living Scales* (ILS) is an individually administered assessment of adults' competence in instrumental activities of daily living. The items, which target situations relevant to independent living, require the examinee to do problem solving, to demonstrate knowledge, or to perform a task. An individual's performance on the ILS can guide determination of the most appropriate living arrangements for adults who are cognitively impaired. Information at the item level is specific enough to identify needed support services, adaptations, or instruction for adults who are unable to function independently in certain areas of everyday living.

Prior to the development of any type of formal assessment, determination of competence was made on the basis of statements from family members or a physician. This practice held grave implications for an individual's liberties and civil rights (Horstman, 1975). There are still very few satisfactory measures of the ability of older adults to take care of themselves or their property (Grisso, 1986, 1994). Most existing measures lack normative, reliability, and validity data (Moye, 1996). Tests of intelligence and neuropsychological assessments have commonly been used to determine competence (Grisso, 1994). Although these tests may provide reliable and valid information about an individual's level of cognitive functioning, they do not directly assess functional competence (Dunn, Searight, Grisso, Margolis, & Gibbons, 1990; Heaton & Pendleton, 1981; Kaplan, Strang, & Ahmed, 1988). Poor results on intelligence tests and neuropsychological assessments do not necessarily mean that a person is incompetent in activities of daily living. Most measures that assess activities of daily living are based on self-report or caregiver report. These measures have questionable reliability and validity because the individual or family member completing the measure may underestimate or overestimate the individual's level of competence, depending upon the reason for the assessment and how well the caregiver knows the subject (Sager et al., 1992; Searight, Dunn, Grisso, Margolis, & Gibbons, 1989; Weinberger et al., 1992). Understandably, a family member may have difficulty being objective about an individual's competence and level of independence. Also, the behavior of the individual whose competence is being questioned must be observed adequately before a reliable and valid assessment can be made. This standard is seldom met even when a family member, a caregiver, or the staff in an institution is doing the rating. Given the serious consequences of decisions concerning an individual's competence, the ILS was created to provide a direct, more objective assessment of functioning in daily life.

Subscales

The ILS is comprised of five subscales: Memory/Orientation, Managing Money, Managing Home and Transportation, Health and Safety, and Social Adjustment. The five subscale scores are added to obtain an overall score reflecting the examinee's ability to function independently. The following list briefly covers the area assessed by each subscale.

Memory/Orientation assesses the individual's general awareness of her or his surroundings and assesses short-term memory.

Managing Money assesses the individual's ability to count money, do monetary calculations, pay bills, and take precautions with money.

Managing Home and Transportation assesses the individual's ability to use the telephone, utilize public transportation, and maintain a safe home.

Health and Safety assesses the individual's awareness of personal health status and ability to evaluate health problems, handle medical emergencies, and take safety precautions.

Social Adjustment assesses the individual's mood and attitude toward social relations.

Factors

Two factors may be derived from some of the items on the subscales: Problem Solving and Performance/Information.

Problem Solving is comprised primarily of items that require knowledge of relevant facts as well as ability in abstract reasoning and problem solving.

Performance/Information is comprised primarily of items that require general knowledge, short-term memory, and the ability to perform simple, everyday tasks.

Clinical Applications

Historically, guardianship proceedings for older adults resulted in a person's being adjudged either fully competent or totally incompetent. Furthermore, when institutionalized, an older adult rarely received treatment but rather mere custodial care. One problem surrounding the global labeling of incompetence has been the gross assignment of guardianship and determination of treatment. For example, the inclusion of "old age" in prior statutory definitions of incompetence conceivably could have resulted in discrimination against older adults. By the early 1970s, legal scholars began to call for statutes specifying behaviors and skills (as opposed to listing diagnoses or labels) to determine incompetence (Alexander &

Lewin, 1972; Horstman, 1975). Because of various abuses stemming from the poor definition of competence, it has been suggested that legal competence no longer be determined by a global diagnosis, but rather by differentiation between areas of strength and weakness. Legal incompetence should be regarded as remediable and considered in the context of the circumstances surrounding a particular case (Grisso, 1994).

The ILS can be used to assess an individual's competence for several purposes. The ILS was originally developed for use with older adults. Questions about older adults' abilities to care for themselves often arise from their own concerns or from the concerns of family members or social service providers. The ILS can be used as part of an assessment to determine if an older adult can manage his or her property and/or personal affairs. Furthermore, the ILS provides information to aid in decision making about the most appropriate living environment and any specific support services required. Annual or periodic evaluations with the ILS can help monitor an individual's improvement or deterioration. In cases where questions arise in court guardianship proceedings, the ILS may be used by the professional to describe an individual's specific strengths and weaknesses with respect to functional competence.

The ILS can be similarly used to facilitate competency evaluations of adults with a psychiatric diagnosis. In the 1980s there was a sharp increase in the number of patients with diagnosed psychiatric disorders who were receiving treatment on an outpatient, as opposed to an inpatient, basis. The shift to community-based treatment resulted in the discharge of patients who were unable without assistance to care for themselves and/or their property. These individuals, like older adults, are increasingly encouraged to live as independently as possible in the community. In general, the ILS may be used with a variety of clinical populations who may be experiencing cognitive impairments, such as individuals with mental retardation, traumatic brain injury, or dementia. The ILS results can help in estimating requirements for community support services and potential for rehabilitation or remediation.

User Qualifications

The administration of the ILS is fairly simple and straightforward. However, an understanding of the importance of standardized administration and scoring is essential. Individuals who administer the test should be knowledgeable about, and experienced in working with, the population they are testing. These individuals may include persons with a bachelor's degree in psychology, nursing, social work, occupational therapy, or a related field. Interpretation of the ILS requires an understanding of individualized assessment as well as knowledge of how to interpret a functional assessment such as the ILS within the context of other clinical information. The individual who interprets the ILS ideally will have completed a master's level program, or the equivalent, that included individual standardized assessment; persons qualified to interpret the ILS may include psychiatrists, social workers, nurses, occupational therapists, and individuals in the field of psychology or in a related field. In general, persons who purchase, interpret, or administer the test should adhere to the criteria set forth by the *Standards for Educational and Psychological Testing* (Committee to Develop Standards for Educational and Psychological Testing, American Psychological Association, 1985). No ILS test materials may be reproduced without written permission; the one exception is for the examiner who wishes to provide a copy of an adult's completed protocol to another qualified professional.

▲ Chapter 2

Development and Standardization

Development of the Tryout Version

The tryout version of the ILS was called the *Community Competence Scale* (CCS; Loeb, 1983). The development of the CCS began with a study of guardianship and conservatorship of older adults. This study entailed an in-depth search of the states' legal statutes on guardianship and conservatorship, relevant case law, and legal criticism on the subject. Development of the CCS also involved investigation of two major domains: the ability to care for one's self and the ability to care for one's property. To accomplish this, open-ended interviews were conducted with knowledgeable professionals (probate court judges, lawyers, physicians, psychiatrists, nurses, psychologists, and social workers), as well as with older adults themselves, to elicit their opinions about what they considered to be the critical aspects of a person's ability to take care of himself or herself and/or property.

The acquired information from the literature review and the interviews resulted in the creation of a survey. The survey included two major domains, the ability to care for one's self and the ability to care for one's property; the two domains were comprised of 19 components, each with specific abilities listed underneath to further define the component. For example, Ability to Take Care of Medical Needs was one of the 19 components listed on the survey. One of the six specific abilities listed under this component was Adequate Awareness of Body and Realistic Perception of Health Status. The survey was sent to approximately 1,000 individuals (in the previously mentioned professions as well as in the general group of older adults). The survey first asked respondents to rate each of the specific abilities on a 5-point Likert scale in terms of its degree of importance to the component under which it appeared. In this way, the respondent defined the component according to the abilities deemed most important. The respondent was then asked to rank the importance of each component. Approximately 300 responses to the survey were returned with representation across all groups. In general, there was consensus across all groups as to the importance of the specific abilities and components underlying the domains.

All 19 components were retained, along with the corresponding specific abilities that ranked 2.5 or above on the 5-point scale, to create 19 subscales with 166 items on the CCS. The subscales were Judgment, Emergencies, Acquire Money, Compensate Incapacities, Manage Money, Communication, Care Medical, Adequate Memory, Satisfactory Living Arrangement, Proper Diet, Mobility, Sensation, Motivation, Personal Hygiene, Maintain Household, Utilize Transportation, Verbal/Math, Social Adjustment, and Dangerousness. The CCS was made as ecologically valid as possible. The examinee was required to give an actual demonstration, for example, of his or her ability to comprehend what a bill is, to simulate making a payment for that bill, and to reconcile the account balance.

The CCS items included sensory-motor tasks, general-information questions that assessed factual knowledge or demonstration of an ability, and more complex comprehension questions that assessed ability in reasoning and problem solving. The test items were designed to be open-ended enough to allow for diverse responses, but structured enough to maximize reliable scoring and enhance the objectivity of the CCS. Thus, examinees could exhibit their individual styles and adaptations to situations. The scoring for the items resembled the item scoring of the Information and Comprehension subtests on the *Wechsler Adult Intelligence Scale* (WAIS; Wechsler, 1955). The items that required the adult to perform a task or to have factual knowledge were fairly straightforward and were scored either "0" or "1." Items that required reasoning and problem-solving ability were scored on a 3-point scale so that partial credit could be given.

Tryout Sample

Thirty-six adults over the age of 65 were assessed with the CCS. Of these adults, 12 were identified as living independently in the community (mean age 75.3 years), 12 were living semi-independently in a home for the aged where they received less than one hour of nursing care daily (mean age 83.5 years)[1], and 12 were living dependently in the home for the aged where they received approximately three hours of nursing care daily (mean age 86.5 years)[2]. Of the 36 adults, 26 were female (72%), all were White, 22% were married, and the overall level of education was 10.55 years.

Statistical Properties of the Scale

Reliability

Internal consistency reliability of the CCS Full Scale and of the subscales was calculated using Cronbach's alpha. The alpha for the Full Scale was .93. The alphas for the subscales ranged from .46 to .90. Interrater reliability was calculated using Pearson's product-moment correlation coefficient. The comprehension items were scored independently by two raters for half of the sample. Only the comprehension items were analyzed, because the knowledge/performance items were believed to be so straightforward that the scoring would not be subject to interpretation. The correlation between the two raters' scores was .91.

Validity

A Multivariate Analysis of Covariance (MANCOVA) was calculated to test group mean differences on the 19 subscale scores of the CCS, with age as a covariate because of the differences in age between individuals in the three groups. Using Wilks's Λ, mean differences were found between the groups. No significant difference was found for age. A series of Analysis of Covariance (ANCOVA) was subsequently used to test mean differences between the (three) groups for each of the subscales. Of the 19 ANCOVAs, 13 indicated that there were significant differences. Tukey's HSD (honestly significant difference) was employed to test the differences among the multiple comparisons. Significant differences were found between the Independent and Dependent groups for the Emergencies, Manage Money, Communication, Hygiene, Utilize Transportation, and Verbal/Math subscales. The Independent group differed significantly from the Semi-Independent group on the Communication subscale.

A discriminant analysis was conducted to determine how well the 19 CCS subscale scores could determine correct classification of living status for the adults. Of the 36 adults, 35 were

---

[1] The semi-independent group had meals provided and heavy household chores and laundry taken care of in the home. They otherwise functioned quite independently: they typically bathed and dressed themselves and ambulated to the dining room, to recreational programs, and around the grounds; they could leave the home to socialize with family and friends.

[2] The dependent group required assistance with bathing, dressing, and maintaining their rooms. Recreational activities consisted primarily of passively listening to music. Individuals in this group left the home only under the close supervision of family or friends.

correctly classified according to living status; only one adult from the Dependent group was erroneously placed in the Semi-Independent group.

Use With Adults With a Diagnosed Psychiatric Disorder

An abbreviated version of the CCS was used in a study of adults with a diagnosed psychiatric disorder. The study investigated whether the CCS would differentiate between those who lived in a very structured boarding home and those who lived in minimally supervised apartments (Searight, Oliver, & Grisso, 1983). Significant differences were found between the groups; the residents living in the more highly supervised boarding home had lower CCS scores than did the minimally supervised apartment dwellers. In a second study by Searight (1983), another sample of deinstitutionalized adults with a psychiatric diagnosis was given the CCS. Fifty-two adults were included: 20 lived in a large urban boarding home, 20 lived in urban cooperative apartments, and 12 lived in a rural boarding home. The urban boarding home and the cooperative apartments were comparable to the more heavily supervised and minimally supervised settings, respectively, in the prior study. The rural boarding home was included in the second study to test for a significant difference in CCS scores between urban-living adults and rural-living adults. Although significant differences in CCS scores were found between the urban boarding home residents and the apartment dwellers, no significant differences in CCS scores were found between the urban and the rural boarding home residents.

Standardization

The standardization edition of the CCS, renamed as the *Independent Living Scales*, included 118 items. Seventy-eight percent of the items came from the 166 items on the CCS. Items that were redundant or that had poor interrater reliability were dropped. Some of the 19 CCS subscales were combined to improve internal consistency reliability of the ILS subscales. An additional 24 items were created to improve the reliability of some of the ILS subscales. Also, directions for administering and scoring some of the items were reworded in an effort to improve the reliability. The ILS materials were standardized, and a few were modified to accommodate the standardized format. The standardization edition had seven subscales: Communication, Acquiring and Managing Money, Emergencies, Memory, Physical Care, Household Arrangement and Transportation, and Social Adjustment. Screening items included at the beginning of the ILS assessed physical status in areas such as vision, hearing, and speech. These items were developed from the sensory-motor tasks of the CCS.

Data for the ILS standardization edition were collected between July 1994 and June 1995. Two samples were collected: a nonclinical sample of 590 adults, 65 years of age and older, who had no known clinical diagnoses that would affect cognitive functioning, and a clinical sample of 248 adults, 17 years of age and older, who had various clinical diagnoses.

Description of the Nonclinical Sample

The criteria for inclusion in the nonclinical sample stipulated that adults be fluent in English. Medical exclusions included the acute stage of a serious medical illness, a recent head injury or stroke (less than 6 months prior to testing), dementia, psychiatric diagnosis, or ongoing dependence on alcohol or other drugs. Examinees with medical conditions could be included only if their health had stabilized.

Within the nonclinical sample, data were collected on three groups according to living status: Independent, Semi-Independent, and Dependent. The Independent and Dependent groups were used for setting cut scores and establishing validity (see Chapter 5). Living status was based on the level of assistance required with activities of daily living (preparing meals, taking medications, using transportation, bathing, dressing, toileting, and attending social events), the need for supervision, adult daycare, or skilled nursing, and the person's current living situation. Information for classification was provided by the examinee and was verified, if necessary, by a caregiver. In general, the Independent examinee resided in a private home, either alone or with family, and was capable of all aspects of self-care, including meal preparation, housekeeping, and attendance at social events. Someone classified as living independently might also have been living in a retirement community without utilizing any of its services except the social functions—living there out of convenience rather than necessity. The Semi-Independent examinee was most likely in a supervised living situation, such as a retirement community or a nursing home, as a relatively high-functioning resident who required assistance for some activities of daily living (e.g., housekeeping, medication reminders, meals, transportation, social activities) or needed some nursing or rehabilitation services on a part-time basis. This group also included persons living at home but receiving some assistance from a family member or a visiting nurse. The Dependent examinee may have lived in a nursing home or a rehabilitation hospital or at home with full-time caregivers. In general, he or she required full-time supervision and assistance with most activities of daily living.

The ILS nonclinical sample included 400 older adults living independently, 100 living semi-independently, and 90 living dependently. Each living-status group was stratified according to the adult's age, sex, education level, race/ethnicity, and geographic region. The target percentages for education level, race/ethnicity, and geographic region were based on the 1993 U.S. census for adults 65 years of age and older (U.S. Bureau of the Census, 1993). The following information provides a breakdown of the nonclinical sample according to these variables. More detailed information appears in Tables 2.1 through 2.6.

Age	The nonclinical sample was stratified according to five age groups: 65–69, 70–74, 75–79, 80–84, and 85+.
Sex	The nonclinical sample consisted of approximately 50% females and 50% males.
Education Level	The nonclinical sample was stratified according to four education levels: ninth grade or less (≤ 9) 10th to 11th grade (10–11) high school diploma (or equivalent) to three years of college or technical school (12–15) four or more years of college (≥ 16)
Race/Ethnicity	The percentages of African Americans, Hispanics, Whites, and other racial/ethnic groups (including Asian Americans, Native Americans, Pacific Islanders) were representative of the U.S. population of adults 65 years of age and older.
Geographic Region	The U.S. was divided into four geographic regions in accordance with the U.S. census: Northeast, North Central, South, and West. Figure 2.1 displays these U.S. geographic regions.

Table 2.1. Demographic Characteristics of the Independent Group: Percentages by Age and Sex and by Age and Education Level

		Sex		Education Level			
Age	n	Female	Male	≤9	10–11	12–15	≥16
65–69	80	51.2	48.8	25.0	21.2	43.8	10.0
70–74	80	47.5	52.5	31.2	16.2	43.8	8.8
75–79	80	51.2	48.8	27.5	15.0	46.3	11.2
80–84	80	50.0	50.0	22.5	13.8	53.7	10.0
85+	80	60.0	40.0	28.8	16.2	42.5	12.5
Total	400	52.0	48.0	27.0	16.5	46.0	10.5

Table 2.2. Demographic Characteristics of the Independent Group: Percentages by Sex and Education Level and by Sex and Marital Status

		Education Level				Marital Status				
Sex	n	≤9	10–11	12–15	≥16	Single	Married	Divorced	Widowed	Unknown
Female	208	27.9	17.3	45.2	9.6	6.2	29.8	7.7	55.8	0.5
Male	192	26.0	15.6	46.9	11.5	5.2	68.2	7.3	18.8	0.5
Total	400	27.0	16.5	46.0	10.5	5.8	48.2	7.5	38.0	0.5

Table 2.3. Demographic Characteristics of the Semi-Independent Group: Percentages by Age and Sex and by Age and Education Level

		Sex		Education Level			
Age	n	Female	Male	≤9	10–11	12–15	≥16
65–69	19	52.6	47.4	31.6	15.8	47.4	5.2
70–74	19	63.2	36.8	21.1	10.5	52.6	15.8
75–79	21	47.6	52.4	33.3	14.3	47.6	4.8
80–84	21	52.4	47.6	28.6	14.2	28.6	28.6
85+	20	55.0	45.0	35.0	15.0	30.0	20.0
Total	100	54.0	46.0	30.0	14.0	41.0	15.0

Table 2.4. Demographic Characteristics of the Semi-Independent Group: Percentages by Sex and Education Level and by Sex and Marital Status

		Education Level				Marital Status			
Sex	n	≤9	10–11	12–15	≥16	Single	Married	Divorced	Widowed
Female	54	35.2	7.4	42.6	14.8	20.4	20.4	5.5	53.7
Male	46	23.9	21.8	39.1	15.2	8.7	50.0	6.5	34.8
Total	100	30.0	14.0	41.0	15.0	15.0	34.0	6.0	45.0

Table 2.5. Demographic Characteristics of the Dependent Group: Percentages by Age and Sex and by Age and Education Level

Age	n	Sex		Education Level			
		Female	Male	≤9	10–11	12–15	≥16
65–69	15	40.0	60.0	26.7	20.0	46.6	6.7
70–74	17	41.2	58.8	29.4	5.9	52.9	11.8
75–79	13	76.9	23.1	15.4	7.7	69.2	7.7
80–84	19	57.9	42.1	31.5	21.1	26.3	21.1
85+	26	76.9	23.1	46.1	0.0	38.5	15.4
Total	**90**	**60.0**	**40.0**	**32.2**	**10.0**	**44.5**	**13.3**

Table 2.6. Demographic Characteristics of the Dependent Group: Percentages by Sex and Education Level and by Sex and Marital Status

Sex	n	Education Level				Marital Status			
		≤9	10–11	12–15	≥16	Single	Married	Divorced	Widowed
Female	54	29.6	11.1	46.3	13.0	7.4	13.0	11.1	68.5
Male	36	36.1	8.3	41.7	13.9	16.7	38.9	11.1	33.3
Total	**90**	**32.2**	**10.0**	**44.5**	**13.3**	**11.1**	**23.3**	**11.1**	**54.5**

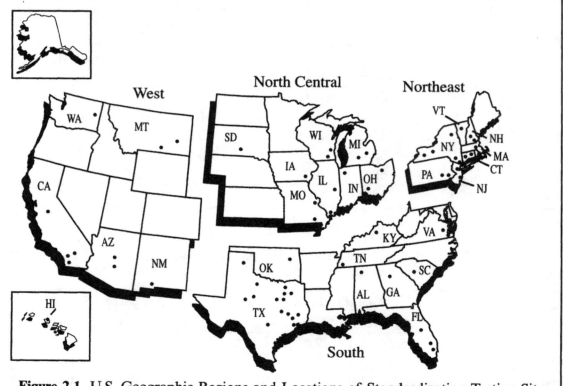

Figure 2.1. U.S. Geographic Regions and Locations of Standardization Testing Sites

Locating and Testing the Sample

Based on the total number of cases needed for the nonclinical sample and the demographic variables used for stratification, a stratified random sampling matrix was generated that provided the target number of adults needed for each cell in the matrix. Examiners located potential examinees in their communities by approaching retirement centers, nursing homes, churches, adult daycare centers, and senior citizen centers to secure adults for the sample. Examinees completed a consent form that included a description of the study and requested the demographic information required to determine whether the adult was needed for the sample. Figure 2.1 displays the location of the testing sites.

Representativeness of the Independent Group

The ILS standard scores are based upon the Independent group. Figure 2.2 demonstrates the representativeness of the Independent group to the U.S. population, ages 65 and older, according to the 1993 census with regard to education level, race/ethnicity, and geographical region.

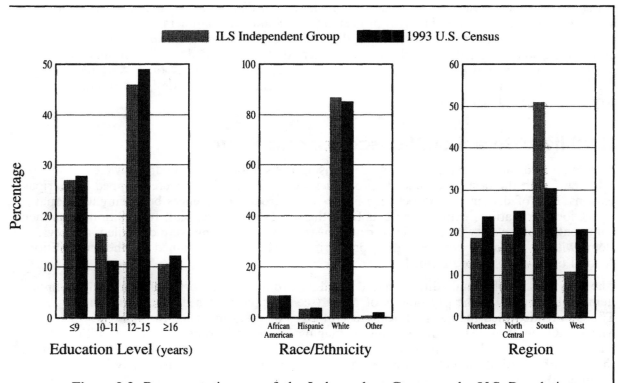

Figure 2.2. Representativeness of the Independent Group to the U.S. Population, Ages 65 and Older

Description of the Clinical Sample

For the purpose of validating the ILS with a clinical population, examiners administered the ILS to 248 adults, each with one of the following diagnoses: mental retardation, traumatic brain injury, chronic psychiatric disturbance, or dementia. Chapter 5 describes the clinical sample in more detail.

Quality Control Procedures

The quality control procedures used in collecting the ILS standardization data were designed to facilitate proper test administration and to ensure that test responses were accurately scored. Examiners were recruited who had training and experience in adult assessment. They possessed at least a master's degree in psychology, or a bachelor's degree in occupational, recreational, or physical therapy, or social work with experience in functional ability assessments. To be selected to participate in standardization testing, prospective examiners completed a background questionnaire that elicited information about their education, the assessment instruments they have routinely administered, licenses or certificates, and professional associations.

All examiners were required to submit their first protocol before receiving approval for further testing. The examiner was required to write down the examinee's responses verbatim. The ILS project staff closely reviewed each practice protocol for proper administration and scoring procedures. Examiners received detailed written and oral feedback on the administration and scoring of their practice protocols. If an examiner committed significant errors on scoring or administration, the project staff asked the examiner to submit a second practice protocol for approval before permitting the start of standardization testing.

All standardization protocols were carefully reviewed for demographic accuracy and proper administration and scoring. The ILS project staff encouraged examiners to call with any questions about administration or scoring directions. Clarifications or changes in administration and scoring were detailed in a series of newsletters that were mailed to all examiners. Items appearing to be scored incorrectly, based on the recorded verbatim response, were rescored by the ILS project staff according to a set of detailed scoring guidelines designed to correct scoring errors made by the examiner.

Final Item Selection, Subscales, and Factors

After standardization testing, all items comprising the standardization edition were examined. The items with the best psychometric properties were selected. Items were dropped for various reasons: lack of discrimination between living-status groups, differences between educational levels, low correlations with other items from the subscale, and sex bias. In addition, examiner comments about clarity of the rules for administration and scoring were compiled and reviewed. Items with no apparent administration or scoring problems were retained for the final edition. A total of 48 items were dropped.

The subscales for the final edition were derived according to a Q sort performed on the final item set by experts in the psychology of aging (see Chapter 5 for a detailed discussion). The Q sort identified the most clinically useful areas of assessment for the subscales: Memory/Orientation, Managing Money, Managing Home and Transportation, Health and Safety, and Social Adjustment. Two factors (Problem Solving and Performance/Information) that contribute additional clinical information were derived from a factor analysis (see Chapter 5).

Bias Analyses

After the final items and cut scores were selected, chi-square analyses were conducted to compare the percentages of females to males who were classified as high, moderate, or low functioning (as defined by the ILS cut scores) within living-status classifications (Independent, Semi-Independent, and Dependent). The total number of females and males were included. There was a significant chi-square ($p < .05$) among only the Independent group on the Memory/Orientation, Health and Safety, and Social Adjustment subscales. For the Memory/Orientation subscale, more males than females were classified as moderate or low functioning. The opposite held true for Social Adjustment, and there were more females than males classified as moderate functioning on Health and Safety.

Chi-squares were calculated to compare the percentages of Whites to African Americans and Whites to Hispanics who were classified as high functioning, moderate functioning, or low functioning according to the ILS. The groups were matched by sex and level of education. The comparisons for Whites and African Americans were performed separately for the Independent group ($n = 35$), and for the Semi-Independent ($n = 11$) and the Dependent ($n = 6$) groups together. These two groups were combined because of their small sample sizes. The chi-square table indicates that significantly more ($p < .05$) Independent African Americans than Independent Whites were classified as low functioning for Memory/Orientation and Health and Safety. There was no significant difference for the Semi-Independent and Dependent groups combined. To compare Whites and Hispanics, the groups were again matched according to sex and level of education. Because there were so few cases (a total of 17 across Independent, Semi-Independent, and Dependent groups), the groups were combined for the analysis. No significant differences were found between Whites and Hispanics on the subscales, the factors, or the Full Scale.

Derivation of Scores

Scores can be computed for the ILS Full Scale, each of the five subscales, and the two factors. The subscale raw score is the sum of all items on that subscale. The factor raw scores can be calculated by adding the item raw scores on each factor, across subscales. A Full Scale raw score per se is not calculated.

Standard scores for adults, ages 65 and older, are provided for the Full Scale, the five subscales, and both factors (see Appendix A). The standard scores are based on only the 400 adults from the Independent group. The five subscales and two factors have standard T scores (a mean of 50 and a standard deviation of 10). The standard Full Scale score is based on the sum of the five standard subscale scores (subscale total sum). The Full Scale standard scores have a mean of 100 and a standard deviation (SD) of 15. All of the standard scores are nonnormalized distributions. The distribution of raw scores was not a normal distribution, nor would it be expected to be normal; the ILS assesses very basic abilities that are minimum requirements for living independently. The distribution of raw scores for the nonclinical Independent group on the Full Scale, the five subscales, and the two factors was negatively skewed; that is, the largest percentage of adults scored above the mean. Therefore, it was considered most appropriate to maintain the shape of the raw score distribution (Crocker & Algina, 1986).

Chapter 3
General Testing Information

Standard Procedures

The directions for administration and scoring of the ILS (see Chapter 4) provide specific information to ensure that each examiner follows standardized procedures. These procedures were used to standardize the ILS and must be followed carefully for the results to be interpreted in relation to the normative data.

Items are arranged within subscales. Begin with the first item for every subscale and administer all items. There are no discontinue rules.

Administration Time

Administering the ILS takes approximately 45 minutes, but testing time can vary considerably, according to the examinee's level of functioning. Make every effort to give the entire test in one sitting. If an examinee becomes uncooperative or is so distressed that proceeding is impossible, stop testing and take a break. Try to complete the testing after the break. If this is not possible, reschedule the completion of the testing for some time within approximately two weeks. During the second session of testing, only items that have not been administered should be presented to the examinee.

Physical Conditions

The testing room should have good ventilation and lighting and should be free from distractions or interruptions. Ideally, you should sit opposite the examinee at a table or desk. If the test is administered at bedside, make sure that the examinee has easy and comfortable access to testing materials. Speak distinctly and naturally to the examinee.

Make every effort to test in a private setting. If an evaluation cannot be conducted privately, firmly discourage the participation of others. Often a spouse or other caregiver will begin to answer for the examinee and greatly affect the examinee's performance.

Test Materials

Many of the materials necessary for administering the ILS are provided in the test kit. The examiner must provide a telephone (disconnected; rotary or push button), a complete local telephone directory, a $10 bill, 6 quarters, 5 dimes, 4 nickels, and 5 pennies, and a stopwatch, scratch paper, envelope, pencil, and pen. When packing the materials in preparation for testing, place the $10 bill, one quarter, and the gray check (separated from the perforated page of the

Record Form) in the pouch with the driver's license, credit card, and key. Figure 3.1 shows all the materials used in administering the ILS.

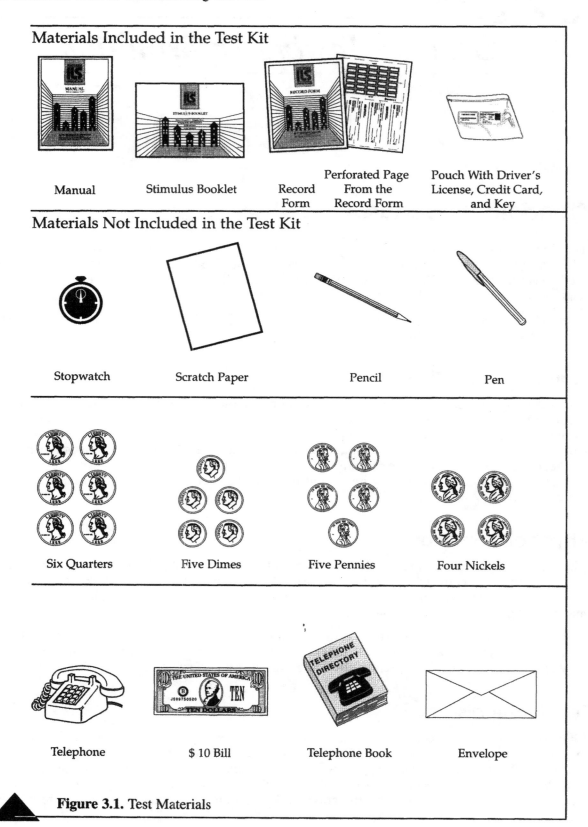

Materials Included in the Test Kit

Manual   Stimulus Booklet   Record Form   Perforated Page From the Record Form   Pouch With Driver's License, Credit Card, and Key

Materials Not Included in the Test Kit

Stopwatch   Scratch Paper   Pencil   Pen

Six Quarters   Five Dimes   Five Pennies   Four Nickels

Telephone $ 10 Bill   Telephone Book   Envelope

Figure 3.1. Test Materials

Establishing and Maintaining Rapport

It is important to establish and maintain a friendly relationship with the examinee. Ask the examinee, "What name would you like to be called by?" Do not address the examinee by using his or her first name unless the examinee suggests it. Using first names may seem disrespectful to those with a formal manner.

To put the examinee at ease, first explain the nature and the purpose of the test. Keep in mind that most older adults have had little experience with any type of psychological assessment. Although the purpose of the test will vary somewhat with each examinee's set of circumstances, the ILS can usually be introduced to the examinee as a series of questions and tasks that are common in day-to-day living. (A general introduction appears in Chapter 4.) Avoid using unclear terms and jargon.

Certain questions, particularly those related to memory function and money management, may create anxiety for the examinee. Reassure the examinee that there may be more than one correct answer and that the important thing is what he or she thinks or feels about the question. If an examinee begins to cry when relating a story or when answering an item on the Social Adjustment subscale, for example, it may become necessary to take a break or even to reschedule the testing. However, if possible, try to go on to the next item.

Some examinees tend to tell stories and to talk beyond giving a response to an item. Be prepared to spend some time in informal conversation with the examinee. During testing be sure to listen to all of the examinee's comments; sometimes a "story" leads to a response, or the response lies embedded in the story. If the examinee is engaging in extraneous conversation after a response has been given, prompt the person back to the task by saying, "Let's go on to the next question."

If an examinee "agrees" or "agrees somewhat" with the statement "I often think of killing myself" (Social Adjustment Item 6), you should evaluate, or have someone who is better qualified evaluate, the examinee's risk potential for committing suicide. Be prepared to provide intervention or to refer the examinee to an individual or agency that can provide intervention. If the examinee is being cared for by another individual or is institutionalized, the caregiver or appropriate staff member should be notified of the suicidal ideation.

Administration of the ILS

Sequence of Screening Items and Subscales

The ILS consists of seven initial screening items and 70 items across five subscales. The screening items assess vision, reading ability, hearing, speech, mobility, ability to sign one's name, and ability to write otherwise. These items are included to provide a structured screening of abilities that could influence the responses to items on the subscales of the ILS. The stimuli for the screening items appear after the Screening divider in the Stimulus Booklet.

Performance on the first four screening items will affect how the test is administered and how the examinee will need to respond. If the examinee cannot hear well enough for the ILS to be presented orally, the section after the Subscales divider in the Stimulus Booklet can be used; it contains item administration for all items in a written format. If the examinee has difficulty reading, even with the help of a visual aid, she or he will have difficulty responding to some of the items that require the examinee to look at a stimulus. In this case, the examinee will not be able to receive full credit for the item; however, this feature reflects the ecological validity of the test. If the examinee knows how to adapt to a circumstance in an area where she or he is challenged, partial credit may be given as directed in the item-scoring directions. If the examinee's speech is so poor that it is incomprehensible, the examinee may write out a response. For some items this may not be practical, in which case the examinee will receive no credit or only partial credit. In order to understand how the examinee might have to adapt to certain situations addressed by items on the ILS, the examiner benefits from knowing the examinee's level of mobility and degree of writing ability (ability just to sign his or her name or ability to write otherwise). In general, the screening information provides insight into challenges that the examinee may face and adaptations that may be necessary to make during testing. The information may also be useful in writing an evaluation of the examinee's performance. Of course, comparable information may be available in greater detail from the individual's medical files.

The subscales appear in the following order: Memory/Orientation, Managing Money, Managing Home and Transportation, Health and Safety, and Social Adjustment. The subscales were arranged in this order to facilitate administration, but it is not essential to administer them in this order. If the examinee can hear well enough for the ILS to be presented orally, the section after the Stimuli divider card in the Stimulus Booklet should be used for administering the subscales.

Item Directions

Each item in Chapter 4 appears with all the information necessary for properly administering and scoring that item. Directions for each item refer to the material(s) needed to administer the item, and include specific instructions for presenting the stimulus materials, time limits for presenting the stimuli—if applicable—and the scoring criteria (see Figure 3.2).

---

❷ 6. Say

> **Let's suppose you are going to the store. I'm going to present you with a shopping list. After I present the list, tell me what you need to buy at the store.**

Open the Stimulus Booklet to Item 6 (showing the shopping list) and place it in front of the examinee.

   orange juice

   cereal

   milk

   coffee

   bread

Allow the examinee to look at the list for approximately 5 seconds and then remove it from view. For an examinee with a hearing impairment, cover the shopping list with the following blank page. For an examinee with a vision impairment, read the list aloud.

   2 points   Correctly recalls the five items (in any order)

   1 point   Recalls 2–4 items

   0 points   Recalls 0–1 item(s)

 Figure 3.2. Example of Item Directions

In most cases, scoring is objective; however, the use of judgment is required for some items. The scoring criteria for each item and examples of examinees' responses are provided but are not meant to be exhaustive. Keep in mind that some responses that are adaptive may be quite idiosyncratic.

Repetition of Items and Probing of Responses

In general, try to get the examinee's optimal performance. Questions or instructions for all items except Items 6 and 8 on the Memory/Orientation subscale may be repeated at the examinee's request or if the examinee does not understand. Encourage the examinee to respond without leading him or her to the correct response, and ask the examinee to clarify any ambiguous or incomplete responses. Permitted probes are "Explain what you mean" or "Tell me more about that." Whenever a response is queried, record a (Q) followed by the examinee's additional reply to indicate that it was not spontaneous. If an examinee gives a response that is followed by a (Q) in the scoring criteria, query for further information or a complete response. Score according to the response given. When two responses are required for a two-point score, query if the examinee gives only one response, regardless of whether the first response was correct. Again, always try to elicit the examinee's best performance.

Idiosyncratic Wording of the Items and Responses

A response that describes an idiosyncratic means of accomplishing a task should be recorded and scored according to the general criteria given for that item in Chapter 4. In addition, responses that are correct because of local circumstances or new technology should be scored as correct. For example, Item 7 on the Health and Safety subscale asks, "If you had pain in your chest, on your left side, and you were having trouble breathing, what would you do?" The response "press my medical alert button" is credited.

Responses that include unusual wording need to be queried to uncover the meaning. For example, Item 18 on the Health and Safety subscale asks, "What would you do if you could not read small print, like the print in the phone book or on the labels of medicine bottles?" An examinee may respond "use a multiply glass" or "get a round circle." Query to allow the examinee to further explain the response. In this example, the examinee was referring to a magnifying glass and received full credit.

Some questions from the Managing Home and Transportation subscale and the Health and Safety subscale may not seem applicable to nursing home patients or to residents of supervised living programs. If the examinee has forgotten that the general instruction is to imagine that she or he is currently living alone, preface these items with "If you were living on your own."

Some individuals may need items with difficult vocabulary reworded. This is permitted as long as the meaning of the item is not changed. For example, Item 7 on the Social Adjustment subscale asks, "What are three things you value in life?" It is permissible to replace "value" with "important to you; mean a lot to you." Item 1 on the Managing Money subscale "How are you supported financially?" may be replaced with "How do you get your money?" In addition, some examinees may need to have the items presented more concretely. For example, Item 6 on the Health and Safety subscale says, "Tell me two ways you would know that it's safe to cross a busy street." It could be rephrased to "You are standing at the corner of a busy street. You need to get across to the other side. How could you make sure it was okay to cross?" In general, rephrase or reword the item to allow the examinee to respond, but make certain that the meaning of the item is not altered. Noting that an item has been reworded is recommended; the information could be useful for summarizing the examinee's performance and making recommendations.

Completing the Record Form

On the inside of the Record Form, space is provided for recording the names of the examiner and the examinee, the date of testing, the examinee's age, and general comments. Space is also provided for recording the raw scores and standard scores. A chart provides a visual representation of scores for the subscales, the Full Scale, and the factors and shows the corresponding level of functioning (see Figure 3.3).

The Record Form provides space with each item so that responses may be recorded verbatim. Score each response on the Record Form by circling the correct score in the Score column. Additionally, if the item is on a factor, the item score should be entered in the space provided, according to whether the item is on the Problem-Solving factor 💡 or the Performance/Information factor ❓. Most items are scored on a 3-point scale (0, 1, 2), but some items are scored on a 2-point scale (0, 2). Criteria are provided in Chapter 4 for each rating on the scale.

Deriving the Raw Scores

To obtain the raw score total for each subscale, add up each item score you circled for that subscale. This number can be entered in the Raw Score box inside the Record Form at the end of each subscale (see Figure 3.3 Ⓐ). To obtain the raw score subtotal for each factor, add up each item score you entered for all items designated on the Problem-Solving factor 💡 or the Performance/Information factor ❓ on that subscale Ⓑ. To obtain the raw score total for each factor, add up each factor's subtotals across subscales.

Deriving the Standard Scores

The standard scores for the subscales and factors can be found in Appendix A, Table A.1. Find the raw score in the Raw Score column and locate the corresponding subscale or factor standard score by reading across that row to the Standard Score column.

To obtain the Full Scale standard score, first add the subscale standard scores to derive the subscale total sum. To locate the Full Scale standard score, find the subscale total sum under the Subscale Total Sum column in Appendix A, Table A.2 and read across that row.

Recording the Scores and Determining the Level of Functioning

Transfer the subscale raw scores and the factor raw scores to the inside cover of the Record Form Ⓒ. Space is also provided for the subscale and factor standard scores Ⓓ, the Subscale Total Sum Ⓔ, and the Full Scale Standard Score Ⓕ. A chart Ⓖ appears below the columns for recording the scores. This chart allows you to record the standard scores and plot a profile in a graphic representation. The chart also indicates the range of scores for each level of functioning (i.e., high, moderate, and low). The cut scores that delimit the levels of functioning for the subscales are indicated by bold black lines on the chart; the cut scores that delimit the levels of functioning for the Full Scale and for the factors are indicated by bold blue lines on the actual Record Form. Where a score falls within a particular range indicates the level of functioning.

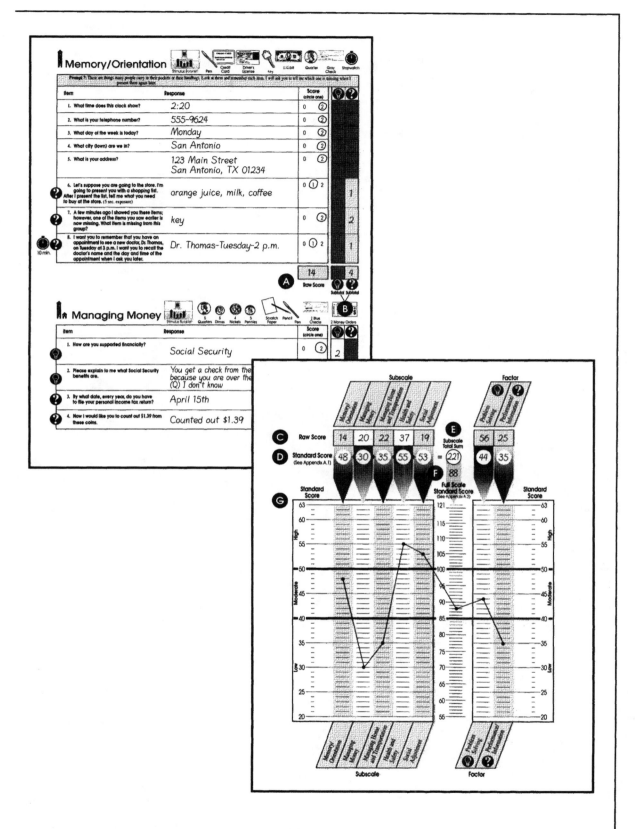

Figure 3.3. Example of Completing the ILS Record Form

Chapter 4

Administration and Scoring Directions

Screening

Materials

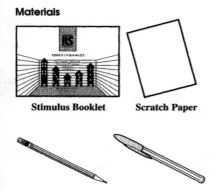

Stimulus Booklet　　**Scratch Paper**

Pencil　　　　　　**Pen**

General Directions

The purpose of the first four screening items is to determine whether the examinee has a vision, speech, or hearing impairment. In some cases, access to a medical history may provide this information. If so, determine which screening items can provide additional information for administering and interpreting the ILS. The Stimulus Booklet is designed for use with adults who can hear and adults with a hearing impairment. The screening portion of the Stimulus Booklet includes written directions that need not be presented if the examinee seems to be able to hear sufficiently. If the examinee's hearing is significantly impaired, however, present each item in print. For the examinee who is visually impaired to a significant degree, read all the test items aloud, except for items that require the ability to see stimuli (e.g., Memory/Orientation Item 1). An examinee who demonstrates significant difficulty in speaking may be instructed to answer in writing. In cases where an impairment exists in one or more sensory modalities, the examinee will not get full credit on some items. Nonetheless, present all possible items and note how the examinee responds. Examinees who cannot perceive the test materials in any of the adapted modes just described and/or who have no means of providing the credited response should not be tested.

The next two screening items assess whether the examinee can sign her or his name and can otherwise write. This information will be useful when writing a clinical report of the adult's abilities and interpreting the performance on some items (see Chapter 6). While the screening items are not given a score or included in any calculation of ILS scores, the responses can be rated as adequate or not adequate. These terms are relative to the administration of the ILS. In general, a score of adequate should indicate that the examinee performed well enough on that item (or that part of the item) to be able to read, hear, see, etc., at that level. On Screening Item 1, for example, the examinee who cannot see well enough to read Item 1a correctly will have difficulty seeing almost all of the ILS stimuli. If the examinee reads only one letter or number incorrectly, the performance should be considered adequate enough to see most of the ILS stimuli. However, as the directions suggest, proceed to administer Item 1b. If an examinee can read only print that is as large as the print of Item 1b, you will have an indication that the examinee can read only if the print is large.

Item Instructions

1. Vision

The examinee may wear glasses or use a personal prosthetic device (e.g., magnifying glass) throughout the exam. If the examinee does use these aids, note them on the Record Form.

Open the Stimulus Booklet to Item 1a, place it in front of the examinee, and say (pointing to the stimulus item)

Please read this aloud.

Write down the letters and numbers that the examinee reads.

If the examinee reads Item 1a correctly (CJA4925), proceed to Item 2a. If the examinee reads Item 1a incorrectly, turn to Item 1b, repeat the instructions, and record the response.

2. Reading

Turn to Item 2a and say (pointing to the stimulus item)

Now read this aloud.

Record verbatim what the examinee says, commenting on any observed reading difficulties.

The examinee should say, "What time does the evening news begin?"

If the examinee reads Item 2a correctly, proceed to Item 3. If the examinee reads Item 2a incorrectly, turn to Item 2b, repeat the instructions, and record the response. Remove the Stimulus Booklet from in front of the examinee.

3. Hearing

Omit Item 3 if the fact that the individual cannot hear has already been established. If the examinee uses some type of hearing aid, note this on the Record Form. The examinee should be encouraged to use the hearing aid throughout the exam. Say

I am going to stand behind you and read a sentence aloud. I want you to say the sentence back to me.

Stand approximately two feet behind the examinee and read, at normal conversational level, the following sentence.

Many people read the newspaper daily.

Record the examinee's response verbatim.

4. Speech

Rate the intelligibility of the examinee's speech, using the following scale. Attend to articulation, vocal volume, and rate of speech.

Circle the percentage on the Record Form that corresponds to the rating assigned to the examinee's speech.

Fully comprehensible	(100%)
Mostly comprehensible	(75%)
Half and half—comprehensible and incomprehensible	(50%)
Mostly incomprehensible	(25%)
Incomprehensible	(0%)

At a rating of 50% or less, it may be necessary to request the examinee to respond in writing.

5. Signature

Place a piece of scratch paper and the pencil or pen in front of the examinee and say

Please sign your name on the piece of scratch paper.

6. Writing

Open the Stimulus Booklet to Item 6 and say

Please write the following sentence.

7. Walking

You can score this item without officially administering it if you have already observed the examinee's walking ability. Otherwise, say

Now I'd like you to stand up and walk forward about six feet, turn around, walk back to your chair, and sit down.

Observe and record what the examinee does (i.e., uses cane or walker; walks with slow or obviously painful movement; shows paralysis, limited range of motion, abnormal posture, or compensatory movements). Also note whether the examinee needs full or partial assistance from another person.

The mode of presentation on subsequent ILS items is based on the examinee's performance on these screening items. Again, if the examinee has a hearing impairment, present items visually, using the section of the Stimulus Booklet that is behind the divider labeled Subscales. If the examinee's speech is comprehensible 50% of the time or less, you may need to ask him or her to respond in writing.

Subscales

General Directions

The scoring criteria provide guidelines for determining how to quantify an examinee's response. Some items have only one response that is correct; other items, however, elicit responses that are much more open-ended. Examples of responses are given to aid in scoring, but the examples are not exhaustive. Decide which of the criteria the examinee's response best fits. In addition, some items require two responses of a particular kind in order to receive the highest score (2 points). If an examinee provides only one response, query the examinee for a second response. In some instances, clinical judgment will be necessary for deciding whether to query. Although guidelines are given for when to query, some responses will be idiosyncratic. If the examinee seems to have misunderstood the question or tends to be reticent, it is best to probe further for a response. In general, the ILS was intended to be sensitive to idiosyncratic responses and to obtain the optimal performance.

Introduce the test to the examinee by saying

Some of the following questions will be easy, and some will be more difficult. No one answers all of them correctly. I want you to answer the best you can; just tell me what you think. When you are answering, assume that you live alone in the community. Sometimes I will say that you should assume you live in an apartment or a house, but in general, just imagine when you answer that you are currently living alone.

▌*Memory/Orientation*

Item Instructions

Prompt 7: Lay out all the materials (except for the Stimulus Booklet and the stopwatch) in front of the examinee while saying

These are things many people carry in their pockets or their handbags. Look at them and remember each item.

(Allow examinees with severely impaired vision to manipulate each item if they wish to do so.)

I will ask you to tell me which one is missing when I present them again later.

Show the items for 1 minute (begin timing with a stopwatch as soon as all the items are positioned in front of the examinee) and then remove them from in front of the examinee.

1. Open the Stimulus Booklet to Item 1 and place it in front of the examinee. Ask

    What time does this clock show?

    The examinee must read the time. Record the time given by the examinee.

2 points	2:20 (± 3 minutes)
0 points	Gives some other time or gives no response

2. Ask

    What is your telephone number?

    If the examinee says he or she has no phone, ask for a phone number where the examinee can be reached. Someone living in an institution may give the institution's number or a previous telephone number. Verify the number with the spouse, caregiver, telephone book, directory assistance, or other source.

2 points	Gives a correct telephone number
0 points	Does not give a correct telephone number

3. Ask

    What day of the week is today?

2 points	Correctly names the day of the week
0 points	Cannot correctly name the day of the week

Materials

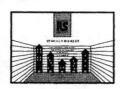

Stimulus Booklet

Pen

Credit Card

Driver's License

Key

$10 Bill

Quarter

Gray Check

Stopwatch

◀ Memory/Orientation

4. Ask

What city (town) are we in?

2 points Correctly names city or town (or nearest one, if in a rural setting)

0 points Cannot correctly name city or town

5. Ask

What is your address?

A person living in an institution may give the institution's address or a previous address. Verify the previous address with the spouse, caregiver, telephone book, or other source. If a previous address is given, it should be the address used immediately preceding the examinee's institutionalization.

2 points Correctly states current address of residence

0 points Cannot give correct address

❷ 6. Say

Let's suppose you are going to the store. I'm going to present you with a shopping list. After I present the list, tell me what you need to buy at the store.

Open the Stimulus Booklet to Item 6 (showing the shopping list) and place it in front of the examinee.

orange juice

cereal

milk

coffee

bread

Allow the examinee to look at the list for approximately 5 seconds and then remove it from view. For an examinee with a hearing impairment, cover the shopping list with the following blank page. For an examinee with a vision impairment, read the list aloud.

2 points Correctly recalls the five items (in any order)

1 point Recalls 2–4 items

0 points Recalls 0–1 item(s)

❷ 7. Again, lay out in front of the examinee the pocket or handbag items from the pouch, in the same order and in roughly the same arrangement, but withhold the key. Say

A few minutes ago I showed you these items; however, one of the items you saw earlier is now missing. What item is missing from this group?

2 points Correctly names the missing item (the key)

0 points Is unable to name the missing item

❷ 8. Say

🕙 **I want you to remember that you have an appointment to see a new doctor, Dr. Thomas, on Tuesday at 3 p.m. I want you to recall the doctor's name and the day and time of the appointment when I ask you later.**

Open the Stimulus Booklet to Item 8 and place it in front of the examinee and say

Please repeat: Dr. Thomas—Tuesday—3 p.m.

Continue administering the ILS. Use the stopwatch to clock a 10-minute interval before asking the examinee to recall the doctor's appointment. At that time, record the response in the space provided. (Should you lose track of the time, a prompt on the Record Form will ask for the recall during the next subscale. If the prompt should come before the end of the 10 minutes, continue timing while administering the ILS and wait to administer the rest of Item 8 at the end of the 10 minutes.)

2 points   Correctly remembers "Dr. Thomas—Tuesday—3 p.m."

1 point   Remembers one or two aspects (i.e., name, day, or time) about the appointment

0 points   Cannot recall any information about the appointment

⚑ *Managing Money*

Materials

Stimulus Booklet

5 Quarters

5 Dimes

4 Nickels

5 Pennies

Scratch Paper

Pencil   **Pen**

2 Blue Checks

2 Money Orders

Item Instructions

💡 **1.** Ask

How are you supported financially?

General: Mentions a reasonable source of income

- Social Security
- Salary from work
- Welfare
- Personal savings
- Pension
- Investments, such as stock dividends
- Generous children

2 points   Mentions at least one reasonable source of income

0 points   Fails to mention a reasonable source of income

💡 **2.** Say

Please explain to me what Social Security benefits are.

General: Shows reasonable knowledge of Social Security

- Monthly benefit check from the government
- Government checks received after 62 or 65 years of age
- Received because payments were taken from previous paychecks
- Support from the government because of disability

2 points   Responds with two or more concepts

1 point   Responds with only one concept

0 points   Cannot describe Social Security benefits

❓ **3.** Ask

By what date, every year, do you have to file your personal income tax return?

2 points   April 15th

0 points   Gives some other date or does not give a date

❓ **4.** Place the coins (5 quarters, 5 dimes, 4 nickels, 5 pennies) on the table. Say

Now I would like you to count out $1.39 from these coins.

Record the response and remove the change.

2 points	Correctly counts out $1.39
0 points	Cannot correctly count out $1.39

5. Ask

About how much does a loaf of bread cost at the store?

2 points	Responds within the range of $0.60 to $3.00 (or appropriate price locally)
0 points	Does not know or gives unrealistic price

❷ 6. Give the examinee a blank piece of scratch paper and a pencil. Say

Suppose you bought a dozen eggs for $1.19. If you gave the clerk $5.00, how much change should you receive? You may use the scratch paper and pencil to do your figuring.

If a calculator is requested, instruct the examinee to answer the item without using a calculator.

2 points	$3.81
1 point	Can tell you how to set up the problem (difference between $5.00 and $1.19) but cannot mentally perform calculation, or makes a calculation error, or states that he or she relies on a calculator after the problem is set up correctly
0 points	Gives some other answer or does not give a response (cannot set up problem correctly)

Prompt: The examinee's answer to the following question determines whether to use checks or money orders in Items 7–10. Ask

Do you use checks or money orders to pay bills?

If the examinee uses checks most often, separate the two blue checks from the perforated sheet in the Record Form and use the checks in Items 7–10. Set the map (from the perforated sheet) aside to use in Managing Home and Transportation. If the examinee uses money orders, separate the money orders and use them to administer Items 7–10.

If the examinee does not pay bills, ask if she or he has ever used a check or a money order. If the examinee has used both, ask which method is most familiar and proceed by asking questions about that method of payment.

If the examinee has used neither, ask

How have you paid your bills?

Record the response for information only and have the examinee answer the appropriate questions from the following section about *either* checks *or* money orders.

💡 7. Ask

Where do you get checks/money orders?

Checks

2 points	Names a type of financial institution
	• Bank
	• Credit Union
0 points	Does not know
	• They come in the mail
	• Someone else gets them for me (Q)

Money Orders

> *2 points*   Names a correct location
>
> - Post office
>
> - Grocery store
>
> - Credit Union
>
> - Convenience store
>
> - Bank
>
> *0 points*   Does not know
>
> - Someone else gets them for me

Prompt: Open the Stimulus Booklet (showing the Social Security check) and place it in front of the examinee. Then hand the examinee the two blank checks or money orders from the perforated sheet, a blank piece of paper, and the pen. Say

> **Record the Social Security check for $320.75 on your scratch paper as the beginning balance.**

Pause and wait for the examinee to do so. The examinee who is unable to write may direct you to do so. If the examinee does not know what to do, discontinue the administration of this item set (Items 8–10) and score each item as 0.

❓8.   Open the Stimulus Booklet to Item 8 (showing the telephone bill). Say

> **Now make out one check/money order payable to the Telephone Company for this bill.**

Wait for the examinee to do so. If the examinee's handwriting is illegible, request that it be read aloud.

Check

> *2 points*   Correctly fills out the check as follows (no check number is required)
>
> - Date (do not penalize if the examinee asks the current date)
>
> - Pay to: Telephone Company (do not penalize if the name of a local telephone company is entered)
>
> - Check amount: $25.00 (written numerically *and* in words)
>
> - Signature (does not have to be legible)
>
> *1 point*   Correctly directs you to fill out the check, or examinee correctly fills it out although handwriting is illegible
>
> *0 points*   Gives incomplete information, no information, or some incorrect information

Money Order

> *2 points*   Correctly fills out the money order as follows
>
> - Date (do not penalize if the examinee asks the current date or if date is excluded)
>
> - Pay to: Telephone Company (do not penalize if the name of a local telephone company is entered; the address may be left blank)
>
> - Examinee's name and address

- Amount: $25.00 (credit is given for *either* writing out the amount *or* printing the numerals)

1 point   Can correctly direct you to fill out the money order, or examinee correctly fills it out although handwriting is illegible

0 points   Gives incomplete information, no information, or some incorrect information

❷ 9.   Open the Stimulus Booklet to Item 9 (showing the gas and electric bill). Say

Now make out a check/money order payable to the Gas and Electric Company for this bill.

Wait for the examinee to do so. If the examinee's handwriting is illegible, request that it be read aloud.

Check

2 points   Correctly fills out the check as follows (no check number is required)

- Date (do not penalize if the examinee asks the current date)

- Pay to: Gas and Electric Company (do not penalize if the name of a local gas and electric company is entered)

- Check amount: $39.50 (written numerically *and* in words)

- Signature (does not have to be legible)

1 point   Correctly directs you to fill out the check, or examinee correctly fills it out although handwriting is illegible

0 points   Gives incomplete information, no information, or some incorrect information

Money Order

2 points   Correctly fills out the money order as follows

- Date (do not penalize if the examinee asks the current date or if date is excluded)

- Pay to: Gas and Electric Company (do not penalize if the name of a local gas and electric company is entered; the address may be left blank)

- Examinee's name and address

- Amount: $39.50 (credit is given for *either* writing out the amount *or* printing the numerals)

1 point   Correctly directs you to fill out the money order, or examinee correctly fills it out although handwriting is illegible

0 points   Gives incomplete information, no information, or some incorrect information

❷ 10.   Say

Now I want you to deduct the two checks/money orders from the beginning balance and tell me how much money, if any, you will have left over. You may use the sheet of scratch paper to do your figuring.

2 points $256.25

1 point   Examinee correctly sets up the problem or correctly tells you how to set it up but is unable to calculate mentally, makes an error, or states that he or she relies on a calculator after the problem is correctly set up

33

0 points   Does not know the correct procedure (if the examinee has written one of the checks/money orders out for the wrong amount and then uses that amount in this question, the score is 0 points, even if that problem is solved correctly)

Prompt 8: Say

Please tell me what you remember about the appointment with the doctor.

11. Say

Tell me two reasons why it is important to pay your bills.

General: Mentions important reasons

- To establish and maintain credit
- To ensure the continued delivery of goods and services
- Moral responsibility to pay your bills
- To avoid penalties such as interest charges
- To avoid legal ramifications

2 points   Responds with two or more general ideas

1 point   Responds with one general idea

0 points   Does not know or denies that it is important

- Don't pay them

12. Say

Name one thing you can do to keep from being cheated out of your money.

General: Recognizes reasonable strategies to safeguard one's money

- Count change
- Read fine print
- Get competitive bids for work
- Don't loan money
- Comparison shop
- Keep records
- Don't pay for services beforehand
- Check that you're not overcharged
- Get contract details in writing
- Write a check for a receipt
- Check on who you are doing business with
- Keep your financial situation confidential
- Don't fall for telephone scams
- Have a will
- Consult a lawyer for business deals

- Don't give out credit card number or Social Security number to solicitors

2 points   Mentions one approach to avoid being cheated

0 points   Is unable to conceive of an approach to avoid being cheated or mentions an ineffective method

- Keep it hidden
- Keep it in a safe place
- Hold onto your pocketbook
- Use traveler's checks
- Never carry money with you
- Put money in a bank
- Don't flash money around
- Be careful (Q)
- Don't know

13. Ask

What is health insurance?

2 points   Explains that if a person has medical problems, the insurance company pays all or part of the costs or bills (also give credit if Medicare or Medicaid benefits are explained correctly)

- You pay the company money each month; then if you get sick they pay part of the medical bill after the deductible
- If you get sick, it pays part of your bill

0 points   Cannot explain correctly

- It means you can go to the hospital or doctor (Q)
- Everyone should have it (Q)

14. Give the examinee a blank piece of scratch paper and pencil. Say

Suppose you receive a medical bill for $350.00. If your medical insurance pays 80% of this bill, how much do you owe? You may use the scratch paper to do your figuring.

If the examinee simply says 20%, ask for the dollar amount. If the examinee appears to have difficulty remembering the numbers, repeat the question and encourage the examinee to write down the numbers.

2 points $70.00

1 point   Correctly sets up the problem or correctly tells you how to set it up but is unable to calculate mentally, makes an error, or states that she or he relies on a calculator after the problem is correctly set up

0 points   Does not know the correct procedure

15. Ask

Why is it important to read carefully and fully understand any document before signing it?

2 points   Recognizes that voluntarily signing a document could make a legally binding contract that could significantly impact one's personal and/or financial status

- You could obligate yourself to payments or lose your house
- You could be agreeing to give up control over your assets
- You should understand what you're signing in case something is written in the fine print

1 point   Expresses partial comprehension of legal or practical impact of signing such a document

- It could get you in trouble (Q)
- They could put me in a home (Q)
- You could get cheated (Q)
- To be protected (Q)

0 points   Does not know its importance or denies its importance

- It's just a piece of paper
- It doesn't matter
- You just should (Q)

16. Ask

What is the purpose of a will?

2 points   Conveys the general idea that a will allows the individual to specify how his or her estate and/or care (living will) will be handled

- You can choose the people who will inherit your assets
- There's a better chance things will be the way you want them to be if you put it in writing

1 point   Relates a specific instance of what a will might contain

- Can make sure my daughter gets the house
- My brother's wife made sure that he left nothing to my side of the family

0 points   Does not know the purpose of a will

- Don't know
- There's no reason

17. Ask

What is home insurance?

2 points   Explains that if anything happens to the home (theft, fire, etc.), the insurance company reimburses the policyholder

- You pay a fee every month and then if you are robbed they will pay you for your losses

- If you have a fire, the insurance company will pay you to replace your damaged items

0 points   Is unable to explain correctly

- It works when you have a flood (Q)

- Don't know

🏙 *Managing Home and Transportation*

Materials

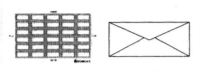

Map

Envelope

Telephone Book

Telephone

Scratch Paper

Pencil

Pen

Item Instructions

For a few items it may be necessary to remind some examinees to respond as if they were living on their own.

💡 **1.** Ask

How would you go about getting repairs made to your home?

2 points   Mentions a reasonable plan for having the repairs made; monitors condition of home

- Notify landlord
- Hire someone to fix things
- Do it myself
- Ask my son-in-law, neighbor, relative, etc., to fix it

1 point   Family member or someone else monitors condition of home and takes responsibility

- Somebody else takes care of it; I don't have to worry about that

0 points   Does not know

- I'm too old and it's too old to worry about

💡 **2.** Ask

What might you do if both your lights and TV went off at the same time?

2 points   Investigate the situation *and*, if necessary, call for help

- Light a candle and see if I could do anything; if not, I'd call the power company
- Check to see if it was just my house. If it were the whole block, I'd light some candles and sit tight
- Check the fuse box

1 point   Immediately call for help without investigating the situation, or merely adapt to the situation

- Call for help
- Light a candle or get a flashlight
- Unplug appliances
- Call the electric company

0 points   Does not know

- Just stay put (Q)
- Go to bed

3. Ask

What would you do if your home was always very hot or very cold?

2 points   Describes a long-term solution to the problem

- Talk to the landlord and get necessary repairs done
- Call a repair person to check the heating or cooling system
- Put in additional insulation, such as plastic on windows
- File a complaint with an agency or go to court

1 point   Proposes a short-term solution to the problem

- Readjust the thermostat
- Layer clothing or take clothing off
- Open or close windows or doors

0 points   Is unable to propose a solution

- Don't know
- Nothing can be done about it (Q)

4. Ask

What are two routine tasks that you do at home, but less often than every day?

2 points   Mentions any two tasks

- Wash clothes
- Take out garbage
- Dust
- Vacuum
- Pay bills

1 point   Mentions any one task

0 points   Is unable to mention one task

5. Ask

Why do we need keys?

2 points   Relates the use of keys and locks to the general concept of security of person or property

- Lock my doors so no one can come in
- So nobody can steal my car or valuables
- For safekeeping

1 point	Mentions a specific use of keys

- To lock our house (Q)
- To start my car
- Open my car door

0 points	Does not know of a use or makes a comment contrary to needing keys

- Just leave my door unlocked
- I don't use keys

❷ 6. Ask

What information can you get from a bus schedule?

2 points	Mentions two or more facts

- Route the bus follows
- When the bus arrives
- Where the bus stops at a destination
- How much it costs to ride

1 point	Mentions one fact
0 points	Does not know

❼ 7. Ask

How would you find out how much it costs to ride the bus?

2 points	Checks with a reliable source

- Call the bus company
- Ask the bus driver before boarding the bus
- Check the bus schedule

1 point	Checks with someone who might know

- Ask my sister, brother, son, etc.
- Ask someone at the bus stop

0 points	Does not know

- Wouldn't go if I didn't know
- Don't know how to find out

❽ 8. Ask

Suppose a person got into a cab and said, "Take me to my daughter-in-law's." What is the problem with that request?

2 points	Understands the problem

- The taxi driver doesn't know the daughter-in-law or where she lives
- No address is given to the driver

1 point	Partially understands the problem

- He might not know where she lives (Q)
- He doesn't know the daughter-in-law

0 points Does not see the problem

- Her house isn't far away

9. Say

Suppose you called a cab to take you someplace. What would you do if the cab didn't come and it was getting late?

2 points Takes action to get a cab

- Call the same cab company again and ask about the service
- Call another cab company

1 point Relies on someone else or becomes late

- Have someone call them for me
- Call a friend or family member to take me
- Call my appointment to let them know I was running late

0 points Does not know

- Guess I really wasn't supposed to go
- Nothing

10. Tear the map from the perforated sheet in the Record Form and hand it to the examinee. Say (pointing to the house)

Assume that your home is the dark block on the map. I want you to trace one of the shortest routes you could take to the grocery store if the store were three blocks north and two blocks west of your home.

If the examinee asks where the store is, answer that the store is on the northwest corner of the block. If the examinee has trouble remembering the directions, he or she may write them down on the scratch paper. After the examinee has completed the task, remove the map and record the response.

2 points Examinee traces one of the shortest routes (see Figure 4.1)

1 point Examinee can verbally direct you to draw the line

0 points Examinee is unsuccessful in tracing or describing the route

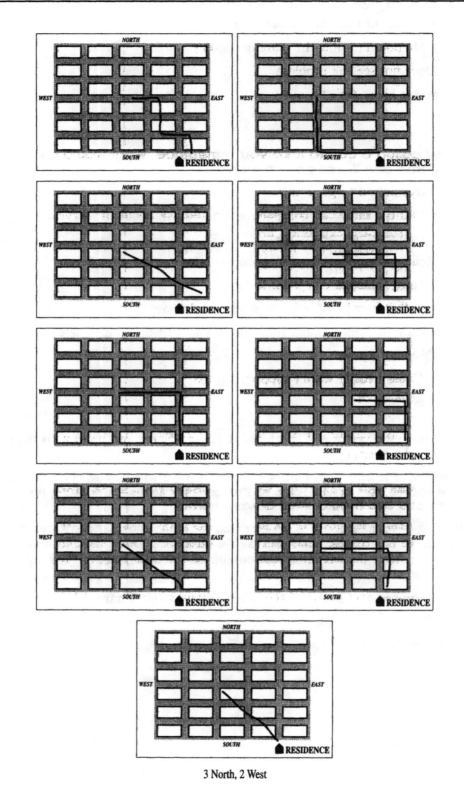

3 North, 2 West

Figure 4.1. Examples of 2-Point Responses

❓11. Give the examinee a blank envelope and a pen. Say

Address this envelope to someone you know. Write all the necessary information on the envelope.

If the examinee cannot remember an example, instruct him or her to make up one or to use his or her own name and address.

2 points	Includes all of the information in this address format

- a person's name

- a number and street (or rural route, etc.)

- a city and state (omission of zip code is permissible)

Give full credit if all the information is included in the appropriate order and in a format that approximates the conventional layout of an addressed envelope. If the examinee omits something other than the zip code, inquire; there may not be a street number in rural areas, for example.

1 point	Can direct you to write a correct address but is unable to write without assistance; completes correctly, but handwriting is illegible; address is written out correctly, but on the wrong part of envelope (e.g., bottom corner)
0 points	Fails to include a person's name, a number and street, or a city and state

❓12. Look in the telephone book prior to testing to verify that there is a common name such as Robert Smith. If there is not, substitute another common first name for Robert. If necessary, use another common surname. Hand the examinee the telephone book and say

I'm going to write down the name of someone whose telephone number I want you to look up. Show me the number when you find it.

If there are multiple listings for the same name, pointing to any of them is correct. However, if the examinee asks which one you want, ask for the first one.

2 points	Points to a correct listing
1 point	Can direct you through the correct steps in locating the listing, but is unable to carry out this task without physical assistance
0 points	Cannot find the telephone number, even with physical assistance

❓13. Place the telephone in front of the examinee (unplug the telephone if necessary). Say

Now I want you to dial that telephone number.

If the examinee was unable to use the telephone book, write down the telephone number on a piece of paper so that the examinee can dial the number.

2 points	Dials correctly
1 point	Dials the Operator and has the Operator place the call

- I don't dial. I tell the Operator that I have a vision problem, and she places the call. (In this case, observe the person dialing the Operator for assistance and requesting that the call be placed.)

0 points	Cannot dial either the number or the Operator, or dials incorrectly

💡 **14.** Ask

Without a telephone book, how could you find a telephone number?

2 points   Responds with a correct service or provides a correct number

- Call Directory Assistance
- Call the Operator
- Call Information
- Dial 411; (1) 411; 555-1212; area code plus 555-1212
- Dial 0

1 point   Relies on someone else to find the number

- Call a friend
- Get someone else to do it

0 points   Does not know how or gives an incorrect number

- Don't know
- Just wouldn't call
- Dial 114
- Remember it
- Find another telephone book (Q)
- Call the phone office

❓ **15.** Say

Show me how you call the Operator.

2 points   Dials 0

1 point   Can direct you to dial 0, but is unable to dial without assistance

0 points   Does not know

Materials

Telephone

Health and Safety

Item Instructions

For a few items it may be necessary to remind some examinees to respond as if they were living alone.

1. Say

Show me how you call the police.

2 points	Dials 911 or the number of the local police station (the examinee is allowed to find the number in the telephone book)
1 point	Can direct you to dial the correct number but is unable to dial without assistance
	Calls the Operator and asks for the police
0 points	Does not know how to contact the police

2. Ask

If you didn't have a regular doctor and you needed medical help quickly, how could you get it?

2 points   Indicates a plan to get immediate medical care

- Go to the emergency room
- Go to the hospital or an emergency clinic
- Call an ambulance or 911
- Press medical alert button

1 point   Describes action that would eventually lead to receiving care, but would not be as immediate

- Call my daughter, son, neighbor, etc.
- Ask my friend who her doctor is

0 points   Indicates no plan of action to obtain medical care

- Wait for my son, neighbor, etc., to come by
- Lie down

3. For the visually impaired, substitute *smelled* for *saw* in this item. Say

Suppose you were outside in your yard and you saw (smelled) smoke coming out of your kitchen window. What would you do?

2 points   Evaluates the seriousness and risks of the situation, then takes appropriate action

- Quickly assess the situation and if necessary, call for help

- If it was a big fire, I'd go next door and call the fire department
- See if it was out of control and try to find out if anyone was inside

1 point Takes action without evaluating seriousness of the situation

- Try to put it out
- Call the fire department
- Use my fire extinguisher to put it out

0 points Reacts without the idea of taking responsible action

- Scream
- Nothing
- Cry
- Run

4. Say

Suppose you are home alone and not expecting anyone. There is a knock on your door about ten o'clock at night. What would you do?

For examinees with hearing impairment, allow for very different responses based on their means of adaptation. Base the scoring on the level of precaution taken.

2 points Indicates awareness of taking maximum precautions

- Ask "Who's there?" and if I knew who it was, I'd let them in
- Look through the peephole to see who it is

1 point Mentions taking precaution, but misses something that would ensure more safety, or overreacts to the situation

- Ask what they want and try to recognize the voice
- Open the door, but with the chain on
- Don't answer the door, it could be dangerous
- Call the police

0 points Reacts in a helpless fashion or shows no recognition that effective precautions should be taken

- Cry
- Open the door
- Nothing (Q)

5. Ask

What are two precautions you can take to protect yourself when going out at night?

General: Mentions reasonable precautions

- Go out accompanied
- Carry money deep in pocket, in a secure bag, etc.

Health and Safety

- Be alert, on guard, and vigilant
- Stick to populated places and routes
- Take my guard dog or attack dog with me
- Wear light-colored clothing or reflectors
- Keep money concealed

2 points   Reports two reasonable precautions

1 point   Reports one reasonable precaution

0 points   Does not know any reasonable precautions or denies need for precaution

- No one would hurt me
- Wouldn't ever go out at night (Q)
- Wouldn't take any precautions

6. Say

Tell me two ways you would know that it's safe to cross a busy street.

General: Mentions safety precautions for crossing the street

- Look at the traffic light or the pedestrian signal
- Look both ways

For visually challenged:

- Listen for cars
- Ask someone else
- Let my guide dog lead me

2 points   Mentions two ways to know it's safe

1 point   Mentions one way to know it's safe

0 points   Does not have a plan for safely crossing the street or does not go out

7. Ask

If you had pain in your chest, on your left side, and you were having trouble breathing, what would you do?

2 points   Mentions immediate attention to, and action on, the pain, including getting to a doctor or hospital

- Call or have someone else call an ambulance or 911
- Press medical alert button
- Take a nitroglycerin pill and if that doesn't work call 911

1 point   Mentions attention to the pain, but suggested action is not as appropriate or immediate

- Call someone (relative or friend) who might know what to do
- Take a nitroglycerin pill (Q)

0 points	Disregards or is unaware of possible seriousness of situation

- Go lie down
- If it didn't go away in a day or two, I'd call the doctor
- Nothing

8. Say

Suppose you smelled a gas odor in the house. What would you do?

General: Ensures personal safety

- Open the windows
- Leave immediately
- Shut off the gas

General: Notifies proper authorities

- Call the gas company
- Call the police
- Call 911
- Call the apartment manager

2 points	Mentions both types of general ideas
1 point	Mentions one type of general idea
0 points	Cannot articulate any effective plan

- Don't light a match
- Look for the source of the leak

9. Ask

If you accidentally cut your hand and it was bleeding badly, what would you do?

General: Treat the cut appropriately

- Apply appropriate first aid
- Put pressure on the wound and bandage it

General: Get professional help

- Phone someone to take me to the hospital, clinic, doctor's office, etc.

2 points	Mentions both types of general ideas
1 point	Mentions one type of general idea
0 points	Does not take appropriate action

- Do nothing
- Wash in warm water
- Put a bandage on it (Q)
- Wait for the bleeding to stop
- Put ice on it

10. Say

Tell me three things that are important to do to take good care of your body.

General: Mentions reasonable things people can do to care for their bodies

- Eat properly
- Take your medication
- Get adequate sleep
- Exercise
- Take a bath or shower
- Go see a doctor when necessary

2 points   Mentions three important activities

1 point   Mentions one or two important activities

0 points   Is unable to mention one important activity

11. Say

Tell me two things about the condition of your health during the past 5 years.

General: Mentions possible health conditions

- I'm strong now, but my endurance is not as good as it was
- Gained too much weight
- Get short of breath
- I've kept my cholesterol level stable

2 points   Mentions two changes, either positive or negative, or mentions two ways in which health remained stable

1 point   Mentions one change, either positive or negative, or mentions one way health remained stable

0 points   Is unable to mention either a positive or a negative change

12. Ask

If you unintentionally lost 10 pounds in 4 weeks, what would you do?

2 points   Recognizes the potential seriousness of the situation and takes appropriate action

- Go see the doctor; even though I didn't feel bad, I might be sick

1 point   Acknowledges weight loss, but suggested action is not as appropriate

- Talk to a friend about it
- Start eating or try to gain weight back

0 points   Gives no recognition of the significance of weight loss

- Nothing
- That's great; could afford to lose a few pounds

Health and Safety

13. Say

Let's suppose you have to take medication three times a day. How would you remember when to take it?

2 points   Gives reasonable plan for remembering to take medication

- Set up three cups with the proper dose in the morning
- Write down the time I'm supposed to take the medication
- Place it out on the counter where I can see it
- Take it with every meal

1 point   Relies on family member or other to remind or assist him or her

- My wife tells me when I need to take my medication

0 points   Is unable to state a plan for remembering to take medication

14. Ask

Why is it important to know about the side effects of the medicine you are taking?

2 points   Indicates that medicines can cause problems, and if these problems arise, the person should know to consult his or her doctor to prevent other difficulties

- If I start feeling sleepy all the time, or depressed, I need to call my doctor
- So you can notify your doctor and get a different medicine if you have a bad reaction

1 point   Only indicates awareness of what side effects are

- Medicine can sometimes make you sick
- So you'll be prepared for the effects
- So you know if you shouldn't be driving or drinking alcohol while taking the medicine

0 points   Doesn't know or cannot describe appropriately

- You're not getting the right medication
- Medicine isn't good for you

15. Say

Tell me two reasons why bathing is important.

General: Indicates awareness of physical health considerations

- It's not healthy to refrain from bathing
- Keep yourself clean (Q)

General: Indicates awareness of social acceptability

- People won't tolerate you for long
- People would smell you

2 points   Mentions both general ideas

1 point   Mentions one general idea

0 points   Does not know or denies importance of bathing

16. Say

Tell me two safety precautions you can take when bathing or showering.

General: Mentions safety precautions

- Precaution against slipping in shower, tub, or on bathroom floor—use mats, etc.
- Guard against falling asleep in the bathtub
- Be wary of water temperature
- Install handles or bars to hold on to
- Keep any electrical appliances away

2 points   Mentions two or more safety precautions

1 point   Mentions one safety precaution

0 points   Does not know

17. Ask

What would you do if you couldn't hear most conversation?

2 points   Suggests a permanent solution

- Have my hearing checked
- Get a hearing aid, if that would help
- Turn up my hearing aid

1 point   Suggests a temporary solution

- Ask people to speak up

0 points   Does not suggest a solution

- Don't care if I can't hear any more; I'm not interested in what most people have to say

18. Ask

What would you do if you could not read small print, like the print in the phone book or on the labels of medicine bottles?

2 points   Mentions a fairly permanent remedy for the problem

- Get a magnifying glass and have it on hand for such occasions
- Get special labels for the bottles with bold print
- Get reading glasses
- Have my eyes checked

1 point   Mentions a temporary remedy for the problem

- Have someone read it to me

0 points   Does not know

- Don't need to do those things

19. Say

Suppose you injured your hip, and the doctor told you it would take much effort and months of physical therapy to be able to walk again. What would you do?

2 points   States that he or she would get the best physical therapy possible and do everything in order to be able to walk

- Go to physical therapy and do everything they told me to

1 point   Makes halfhearted statement about cooperating with rehabilitation

- Try to walk
- Guess I'd take the therapy

0 points   Would not take any action to walk again

- Don't need to walk anymore
- Wait it out

20. Ask

What are two dangers of staying in bed all the time?

General: Mentions physical or mental problems

- It's not healthy
- Might get bed sores
- You'd get weak
- Make you lazy
- Get depressed
- Wouldn't be in contact with anyone

2 points   Mentions two ideas

1 point   Mentions one idea

0 points   Does not know or denies that staying in bed could be harmful

Materials

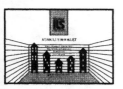

Stimulus Booklet

Social Adjustment

Item Instructions

Prompt: Place Stimulus Booklet, opened to Item 1, in front of the examinee. Say (pointing to the stimulus item)

Use this scale to rate this statement. 1 means *Agree*, 2 means *Agree somewhat*, and 3 means *Disagree*. Let's try the first one.

For an examinee with a hearing impairment, show the written explanation of the rating scale in the Stimulus Booklet.

1. Say

   I look forward to tomorrow.

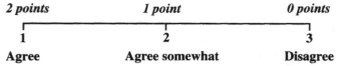

2. Say (pointing to the stimulus item)

   I feel good about myself.

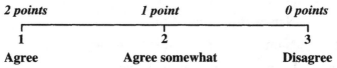

3. Say (pointing to the stimulus item)

   Now rate this statement: I always feel "down."

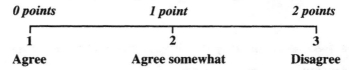

4. Say (pointing to the stimulus item)

   I am often angry at others.

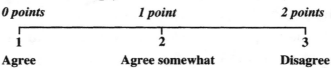

5. Say (pointing to the stimulus item)

   I feel I would be missed if I weren't around anymore.

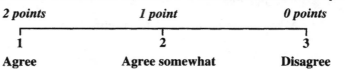

6. Say (pointing to the stimulus item)

Please rate this statement: I often think of killing myself.

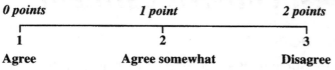

0 points   *1 point*   *2 points*

     1   2   3

   Agree   **Agree somewhat**   **Disagree**

7. Ask

What are three things you value in life?

General: Mentions valued things

- Spouse
- Hobby
- Children
- Job
- Friends
- Grandchildren
- Money
- Home
- Pet

2 points   Names three valued things

1 point   Names one or two valued things

0 points   Is unable to name one valued thing
- Nothing matters
- Don't know

8. Say

Tell me two reasons why it is important to have relationships with people.

General: Mentions reasons to have relationships

- The people you're involved with can help you when you need it
- Other people may give you a lot of good ideas and help you out
- It's good to have someone to talk to
- You do things with people, and it's important to remain active

2 points   Mentions two reasons

1 point   Mentions one reason

0 points   Is unable to state a reason
- Don't like people
- Everyone is only out for themselves

Social Adjustment

9. Ask

How often do you talk to a friend?

2 points   Reports at least once per week

1 point   Reports at least once per month

0 points   Reports less than once per month

10. Ask

How often do you see this friend?

2 points   Reports at least every other week, or less frequently, but explains that they live a considerable distance apart

1 point   Reports at least once per month

0 points   Reports less than once per month

Chapter 5

Statistical Properties

Reliability

The reliability of a test refers to its precision and consistency of measurement and to the stability of its scores over time. This chapter includes a discussion of the various methods used for establishing reliability for the ILS.

Internal Consistency Reliability

The internal consistency reliability was calculated on the five ILS subscales, the two factors, and the Full Scale. The calculation included all 590 nonclinical cases. The reliability was calculated using coefficient alpha, a conservative estimate of internal consistency reliability. Reliability is lowest for the two subscales that have the fewest items (Memory/Orientation and Social Adjustment), although the alphas still indicate a high level of internal consistency. The other three subscales, the two factors, and the Full Scale all have a high degree of internal consistency. The alpha coefficients for the ILS subscales, factors, and the Full Scale follow.

Subscale	Alpha Coefficient
Memory/Orientation	.77
Managing Money	.87
Managing Home and Transportation	.85
Health and Safety	.86
Social Adjustment	.72
Factor	
Problem Solving	.86
Performance/Information	.92
Full Scale	.88

Test-Retest Reliability

The stability of ILS scores over time was assessed in a study of 80 adults from the nonclinical sample (mean = 77 years of age, $SD = 8$) to whom the test was administered twice. The interval between testings ranged from 7 to 24 days (mean = 14, $SD = 3$). The sample consisted of 60% females and 40% males, and 90% Whites, 9% African Americans, and 1% Hispanics. Living-status percentages of the sample were 39% Independent, 30% Semi-Independent, and 31% Dependent.

Education-level percentages of the sample, as measured by years of schooling, were 30% for 9 years or less, 11% for 10–11 years, 46% for 12–15 years, and 13% for 16 years or more.

Table 5.1 provides the means and standard deviations for the first and second administrations along with the reliability coefficient for each subscale, the two factors, and the Full Scale. Although there was a tendency for the means to be higher for the second administration, there was no significant difference between the means at the first and second administrations. The correlations between the first and second administrations are high (all above .80).

 Table 5.1. Test-Retest Reliability

	First Administration		Second Administration		
	Mean	*SD*	**Mean**	*SD*	*r*
Subscale					
Memory/Orientation	41.2	14.1	45.5	14.6	.84
Managing Money	38.6	12.8	40.9	13.2	.92
Managing Home and Transportation	44.0	12.4	46.3	12.3	.83
Health and Safety	43.6	13.0	46.6	12.4	.88
Social Adjustment	45.8	12.1	47.2	11.2	.81
Factor					
Problem Solving	41.3	12.4	43.6	12.1	.90
Performance/Information	41.7	13.5	44.9	13.9	.94
Full Scale	85.8	20.1	90.3	20.9	.91

Decision Consistency

The test-retest data were analyzed also to determine the stability of classifying an adult as high, moderate, or low functioning according to the ILS cut scores. Stability in classification is the percentage of adults who are classified the same on the first and second administrations. Table 5.2 provides the stability estimates for each level of functioning for the subscales, the factors, and the Full Scale. The Performance/Information factor has the highest stability; this factor classifies individuals at the same level of functioning across administrations, 100% of the time. The Health and Safety subscale also shows a high rate of agreement in classification across time. The ability to classify an adult as high functioning remains highly stable across two administrations for the ILS, except for the Social Adjustment subscale. It would appear that the older adults' attitudes and feelings change somewhat across time. However, the high-functioning adults tended to remain more stable on the Social Adjustment subscale than did the moderate- or low-functioning adults. The scores for moderate-functioning adults are the most unstable across administrations. Roughly half of the moderate-functioning adults improved their performance on the ILS and had scores that fell in the high-functioning range on the second administration. Most of the low-functioning adults remained in that range of functioning, although a small percentage moved up to the moderate-functioning range. This trend reflects the higher mean scores on the second administration and may indicate that adults who are in the moderate- to low-functioning range are able to improve their functional ability with practice in certain areas. These results also imply that test security is important, because "teaching to the test" may be possible, at least to a limited degree. Another explanation is that some older adults may have felt more relaxed during the second administration; hence, the improvement in performance. The first administration may have served as a "warm-up" for older adults unaccustomed to the schema for test taking (i.e., providing as comprehensive an answer as possible and giving a higher order response, rather than specific, concrete answers).

Table 5.2. Test-Retest Decision Consistency: Percentages for Stability Estimates of Levels of Functioning

First Administration	Second Administration		
	High	**Moderate**	**Low**
Subscale			
Memory/Orientation			
High	**92.3**	3.9	3.8
Moderate	62.5	**37.5**	0.0
Low	13.3	13.3	**73.4**
Managing Money			
High	**90.9**	9.1	0.0
Moderate	58.8	**29.4**	11.8
Low	2.4	17.1	**80.5**
Managing Home and Transportation			
High	**91.4**	0.0	8.6
Moderate	57.9	**42.1**	0.0
Low	7.7	26.9	**65.4**
Health and Safety			
High	**94.7**	0.0	5.3
Moderate	45.5	**45.4**	9.1
Low	9.7	12.9	**77.4**
Social Adjustment			
High	**73.7**	23.7	2.6
Moderate	44.4	**44.5**	11.1
Low	4.2	33.3	**62.5**
Factor			
Problem Solving			
High	**96.0**	4.0	0.0
Moderate	41.7	**50.0**	8.3
Low	0.0	22.6	**77.4**
Performance/Information			
High	**100.0**	0.0	0.0
Moderate	0.0	**100.0**	0.0
Low	0.0	0.0	**100.0**
Full Scale			
High	**92.6**	3.7	3.7
Moderate	52.4	**47.6**	0.0
Low	0.0	18.7	**81.3**

Interrater Reliability

Two raters independently rated every protocol from the nonclinical sample ($n = 590$). The raters were trained on the general scoring rules and were given examples of a 2-, 1-, or 0-point response for each item. Three of the items (Memory/Orientation Items 2, 4, and 5) could not be scored by the raters; the examiner's rating had to be accepted because it was not possible for the rater to verify the examinee's response.

The generalizability coefficient was used to report interrater reliability (Crocker & Algina, 1986). The scoring of some of the items is straightforward (i.e., there is only one correct answer). Other items require some explanation or application of knowledge, and although some of these items can be scored fairly objectively, some items call for a more subjective response. These items are presented with general criteria for the 2-, 1-, or 0-point responses, and examples are provided for the scoring criteria. The interrater reliability for each subscale, both factors, and the Full Scale is very high, as shown here.

Subscale	Intraclass Correlation
Memory/Orientation	.98
Managing Money	.99
Managing Home and Transportation	.98
Health and Safety	.96
Social Adjustment	.95
Factor	
Problem Solving	.98
Performance/Information	.99
Full Scale	.99

Validity

Validity refers to the ability of an instrument to measure what it claims to measure. The validity of a test accumulates over the life of its use as a clinical instrument and in research. However, it is imperative to have validity data on an instrument at its inception, as well. There are several different ways to validate an instrument, including content, factorial, concurrent, criterion-related, and construct validity. The following sections describe these types of validity as they pertain to the ILS.

Content Validity

The ILS achieved content validity throughout its course of development. The items and the subscales were developed in accordance with what was identified as important by older adults and by professionals knowledgeable about competency issues among older adults. A Q sort guided the final subscale composition to identify the major constructs of the final edition of the ILS.

After selection of the final item set, a Q sort was sent to four experts in the psychology of aging. These experts were asked to sort the items according to areas of competence (e.g., caring for the physical self) and label those areas. The number of areas of competence produced by the experts ranged from 6 to 12. The number of items assigned to any one area ranged from 1 to 20. Two criteria were used to derive the final subscales. First, items were grouped under a subscale if at least three of the experts placed them under a similarly labeled area. This formed the Managing Money, Social Adjustment, and Health and Safety subscales. (For the Health and Safety subscale, all items except one were agreed upon by three of the four experts.) For the Memory/Orientation subscale, three of the four experts agreed on all but two items, and these two items were agreed upon by two of the four experts. For the Managing Home and Transportation subscale, all but three items met the first criterion (the agreement of three of the four experts); these three items were not identified by an area of competence but rather by an underlying ability such as problem solving. The other criterion was to make each subscale that was based on a functional content area broad enough in scope to be clinically useful and also highly reliable. Table 5.3 reveals the relationship between the Q sort's areas of competence and the final ILS subscales.

Table 5.3. Correspondence Between the ILS Subscales and Experts' Labeled Areas of Competence for a Q Sort

ILS Subscales	Q-Sort Areas of Competence
Memory/Orientation	Memory Orientation
Managing Money	Financial Affairs Finances Financial Managing Financial Affairs
Managing Home and Transportation	Managing Home and Public Transportation Transportation and Mobility Transportation (Getting Around) Communication Telephone
Health and Safety	Safety Health Taking Precautions to Avoid Health and Safety Dangers Responding to Emergencies (Health and Safety) Grooming and Personal Care Problem Solving and Handling Emergencies Health/Medical Self-Care Avoiding Danger and Managing Emergencies
Social Adjustment	Maintaining Social Contacts Social Relations Morale Social Competence Social Skills Mood Ratings

Factorial Validity

An exploratory principal components analysis, conducted using a Varimax rotation, permitted an empirical investigation of the underlying structure of the ILS. The analysis was performed on the nonclinical sample. One major factor was found with an eigenvalue of 17.96. Additional factors were found to have eigenvalues greater than one. Based on the eigenvalues and the perceived interpretability of the factors, 4-, 5-, and 6-factor solutions were explored. The pattern of factor loadings, in relation to the conceptualization of the ILS, determined that the four-factor model best represented the data. Factors 2, 3, and 4, had eigenvalues of 2.48, 2.06, and 1.89, respectively. The first two factors were retained because they provide information not reflected by the subscales. These factors were labeled Problem Solving and Performance/Information. Items included on these two factors have factor loadings of .30 or greater, as shown in Table 5.4.

Table 5.4. Principal Components Analysis

		Item	Factor Loading
Problem-Solving Factor[a]			
Subscale			
Managing Home and Transportation	1.	Home repairs	.59
Health and Safety	16.	Bath safety	.55
Managing Money	1.	Income	.54
Managing Money	15.	Read document	.53
Health and Safety	7.	Chest pains	.53
Managing Money	17.	Home insurance	.51
Managing Money	16.	Will	.50
Social Adjustment	7.	Value in life	.50
Managing Home and Transportation	7.	Cost to ride	.49
Health and Safety	20.	Staying in bed	.49
Health and Safety	11.	Health status	.47
Managing Money	12.	Cheated	.46
Health and Safety	6.	Cross busy street	.45
Social Adjustment	8.	Involved with people	.45
Managing Home and Transportation	4.	Chores	.44
Health and Safety	10.	Important for health	.44
Health and Safety	15.	Bathing	.44
Managing Money	11.	Pay bills	.43
Health and Safety	2.	Medical help	.43
Managing Home and Transportation	8.	Directions to cab driver	.42
Managing Home and Transportation	14.	Find number	.42
Health and Safety	19.	Injured hip	.40
Managing Money	13.	Health insurance	.39
Health and Safety	12.	Lost 10 pounds	.39
Health and Safety	9.	Cut hand	.38
Health and Safety	14.	Why know side effects	.38
Managing Money	7.	From where	.36
Managing Home and Transportation	9.	Late cab	.36
Health and Safety	8.	Gas odor	.35
Managing Money	2.	Social Security	.33
Health and Safety	4.	Knock at door	.33
Health and Safety	13.	Taking medication	.31
Managing Home and Transportation	2.	Lights and TV	.30
Performance/Information Factor[b]			
Subscale			
Managing Money	8.	Telephone Company	.72
Managing Money	9.	Gas and Electric Company	.70
Managing Money	10.	Balance remaining	.68
Managing Money	14.	Deductible	.60
Memory/Orientation	8.	Dr. Thomas	.58
Managing Money	6.	Change	.56
Managing Home and Transportation	10.	Map	.50
Managing Home and Transportation	11.	Address envelope	.49
Managing Home and Transportation	12.	Telephone book	.49
Managing Money	3.	Income tax	.46

[a]The Problem-Solving factor has 33 items. Eigenvalue = 17.96.

[b]The Performance/Information factor has 21 items. Eigenvalue = 2.48.

Table 5.4. Principal Components Analysis *(continued)*

		Item	Factor Loading
Health and Safety	5.	Careful at night	.46
Managing Home and Transportation	6.	Bus schedule	.43
Managing Home and Transportation	13.	Dial number	.42
Health and Safety	17.	Couldn't hear	.41
Health and Safety	18.	Small print	.39
Health and Safety	1.	Police	.38
Memory/Orientation	6.	Shopping list	.37
Managing Home and Transportation	15.	Operator	.36
Memory/Orientation	7.	Missing item	.35
Managing Money	4.	Coins	.31
Health and Safety	3.	Smoke	.31

[a]The Problem-Solving factor has 33 items. Eigenvalue = 17.96.
[b]The Performance/Information factor has 21 items. Eigenvalue = 2.48.

The third and fourth factors closely replicated the Memory/Orientation and Social Adjustment subscales, respectively. These factors were not retained because the information they provided would have been redundant with the subscale scores. Roughly 73% of the items are captured by the first two factors. These factors reflect two of the three item types that were identified on the *Community Competence Scale*; that is, questions that demand complex reasoning and problem solving ability (Problem Solving) and questions that require knowledge of factual information or demonstration of a task (Performance/Information).

Concurrent Validity Studies

As mentioned previously, most assessments of functional competence are distal measures rather than direct assessments of everyday living skills. Tests that assess cognitive abilities are, by inference, expected to predict a person's ability to carry out activities of daily living. The ILS concurrent validity studies include the *Wechsler Adult Intelligence Scale—Revised* (WAIS–R; Wechsler, 1981) and *MicroCog: Assessment of Cognitive Functioning* (MicroCog; Powell et al., 1993) to assess both convergent and divergent validity. Other typical measures of daily living skills have been checklists completed either by self-report or by a caregiver. The Activities of Daily Living Domain (ADL) from the Philadelphia Geriatric Center *Multilevel Assessment Instrument* (Lawton & Moss, n.d.) was chosen as a validity measure because it has been in use for more than 10 years, it is representative of the self-report measures of daily living skills, and it has respectable reliability and validity data reported in the literature. The ADL was used as an assessment to establish convergent and divergent validity with the ILS.

Correlation With the *Wechsler Adult Intelligence Scale—Revised*

The WAIS–R is an individually administered instrument for assessing the intelligence of adults. It is composed of six verbal subtests and five performance subtests. The ILS and the WAIS–R were administered in counterbalanced order to a sample of 90 adults from the nonclinical sample (mean = 77 years of age, *SD* = 8). The time interval between testings ranged from 0 to 36 days (mean = 5, *SD* = 7). The sample consisted of 54% females and 46% males, and 89% Whites, 9% African Americans, 1% Hispanics, and 1% other racial/ethnic origins. Living-status percentages of the sample were 47% Independent, 25% Semi-Independent, and 28% Dependent. Education-level percentages of the sample, as measured by years of schooling, were 27% for 9 years or less, 17% for 10–11 years, 46% for 12–15 years, and 10% for 16 years or more.

Table 5.5 presents the correlations between the two tests. Because of the older ILS sample, the age-corrected norms from Ryan, Paolo, and Brungardt (1990) were used for individuals ages 75 and older. For adults 65–74 years of age, the age-corrected subtest norms were used. The lowest correlations occur between the WAIS–R subtests, Verbal IQ, Performance IQ, and Full Scale IQ and the ILS Social Adjustment subscale. There is a moderately high correlation between the ILS Managing Money subscale and the Arithmetic subtest of the WAIS–R. This reflects the fact that almost one quarter of the items on the Managing Money subscale involve arithmetic. Digit Span, a subtest that assesses short-term memory is the subtest on the WAIS–R that is most highly correlated with the Memory/Orientation subscale on the ILS. The overall pattern of correlations suggests that the ILS subscales assess constructs that are related, but clearly are not identical, to general intelligence as measured by the WAIS–R, and suggests that the ILS Social Adjustment subscale has little relationship to intelligence (within a normal IQ range). Although the WAIS–R and the ILS assess related constructs, the WAIS–R does not provide direct evidence of the individual's ability to perform activities of daily living; the ILS provides information about the specific strengths and weaknesses in the individual's level of functional competence.

Correlation With *MicroCog: Assessment of Cognitive Functioning*

MicroCog is a computer-administered and computer-scored test that assesses neurocognitive functioning in adults. MicroCog combines 18 subtest scores to form nine index scores: Attention/Mental Control, Memory, Reasoning/Calculation, Spatial Processing, Reaction Time, Information Processing Speed, Information Processing Accuracy, General Cognitive Functioning, and General Cognitive Proficiency. (For the purposes of this study, General Cognitive Functioning and General Cognitive Proficiency were excluded because they are less pertinent than the other index scores to performance on the ILS.)

The ILS and MicroCog were administered in counterbalanced order to a sample of 47 adults from the nonclinical sample (mean = 80 years of age, SD = 7). The time interval between testings ranged from 0 to 7 days (mean = .3, SD = 1). The sample consisted of 70% females and 30% males, and 98% Whites and 2% Hispanics. Living-status percentages of the sample were 53% Independent, 32% Semi-Independent, and 15% Dependent. Education-level percentages of the sample, as measured in years of schooling, were 19% for 9 years or less, 8% for 10–11 years, 45% for 12–15 years, and 28% for 16 or more years.

Table 5.6 presents the correlations between the two tests. The MicroCog age-corrected norms were the most appropriate for the ILS sample. There were three 90-year-olds; these cases were compared to the 80- to 89-year-old normative group. Overall, the pattern of correlations suggests that the ILS and MicroCog are assessing somewhat similar constructs. There are high and moderate correlations between Attention/Mental Control and Memory, respectively, on MicroCog and Memory/Orientation on the ILS. Moderately high correlations appear between the ILS subscales (except for Social Adjustment) and factors and the older adult's reaction time (Reaction Time) as assessed by MicroCog, and high correlations exist between the ILS subscales (except for Social Adjustment) and factors and processing accuracy (Information Processing Accuracy) as assessed by MicroCog. Although these abilities are not directly assessed by the ILS, the ability to retrieve the appropriate factual knowledge, as well as the reasoning and problem-solving ability required for the ILS, does appear to relate moderately to attention, integration of stimuli, and the ability to complete simple and complex mental tasks accurately (a few aspects of neurological functioning tapped by the MicroCog subtests). One factor that may attenuate the correlations between MicroCog subtests such as Reasoning/Calculation and an ILS subscale such as Managing Money, which requires the ability to reason and calculate, could be the computerized format of MicroCog. Many of the older adults participating in the ILS standardization were not familiar with using computers or responding within time

Table 5.5. Correlations Between the ILS and the WAIS–R

| WAIS–R | ILS | | | | | | | | WAIS–R | |
	Memory/Orientation	Managing Money	Managing Home and Transportation	Health and Safety	Social Adjustment	Problem Solving	Performance/Information	Full Scale	Mean	SD
Information	.34	.61	.65	.59	.15	.63	.60	.58	9.9	2.9
Digit Span	.42	.56	.57	.50	.28	.52	.58	.56	9.6	2.7
Vocabulary	.30	.58	.65	.53	.11	.56	.60	.53	10.5	3.6
Arithmetic	.34	.66	.62	.60	.19	.64	.61	.61	9.5	3.0
Comprehension	.36	.68	.67	.61	.16	.65	.66	.61	10.6	3.8
Similarities	.34	.60	.67	.53	.19	.58	.60	.58	10.7	3.5
Picture Completion	.29	.49	.57	.49	.13	.46	.56	.49	10.5	3.6
Picture Arrangement	.34	.55	.55	.48	.14	.48	.55	.51	10.5	3.8
Block Design	.35	.61	.61	.52	.29	.53	.61	.60	9.9	3.4
Object Assembly	.35	.51	.55	.46	.21	.45	.57	.53	9.7	3.7
Digit Symbol	.43	.56	.54	.53	.38	.54	.58	.57	9.1	3.6
Verbal IQ	.42	.73	.75	.67	.21	.71	.73	.68	99.9	17.1
Performance IQ	.44	.65	.67	.60	.26	.59	.69	.65	99.2	18.1
Full Scale IQ	.47	.76	.78	.70	.25	.72	.78	.73	99.7	17.4
ILS										
Mean	44.6	40.6	45.3	42.2	46.2	40.4	44.3	87.8		
SD	12.5	13.5	13.2	13.3	11.1	13.3	13.0	20.4		

Table 5.6. Correlations Between the ILS and MicroCog

MicroCog	Memory/Orientation	Managing Money	Managing Home and Transportation	Health and Safety	Social Adjustment	Problem Solving	Performance/Information	Full Scale	Mean	SD
				ILS					MicroCog	
Attention/Mental Control	.75	.60	.55	.68	.45	.65	.68	.72	92.9	21.5
Reasoning/Calculation	.46	.32	.20	.39	.20	.36	.33	.44	97.7	19.3
Memory	.60	.53	.33	.49	.35	.50	.52	.58	99.0	19.9
Spatial Processing	.57	.51	.34	.50	.38	.51	.50	.60	95.6	21.7
Reaction Time	.64	.58	.55	.59	.48	.57	.64	.69	86.8	20.8
Information Processing Speed	−.05	−.15	−.33	−.14	−.28	−.16	−.22	−.10	95.6	17.7
Information Processing Accuracy	.80	.71	.69	.77	.59	.77	.78	.81	93.0	26.1
ILS										
Mean	47.6	44.3	47.5	46.0	43.9	43.2	48.5	93.6		
SD	14.7	12.9	12.7	13.0	14.1	11.6	13.6	20.6		

constraints. This may be evidenced by the low, negative correlations between the ILS subscales, factors, and Full Scale and Information Processing Speed. Again, the ILS is more ecologically valid for an assessment of functional ability in terms of the actual tasks the individual is required to perform.

Correlation With the Activities of Daily Living Domain

The Activities of Daily Living Domain (ADL) is comprised of the Philadelphia Geriatric Center *Multilevel Assessment Instrument*'s Personal Self-Maintenance Scale and Instrumental Activities of Daily Living Scale for a total of 16 items (Lawton & Moss, n.d.). The ADL asks the examinee to use a 3-point scale (without help, with some help, not at all) to rate how well she or he can perform activities such as using the telephone, preparing meals, doing housework, managing money, bathing, and toileting. The items on the ADL share most of their content coverage with the Managing Home and Transportation subscale and the Health and Safety subscale on the ILS. For the purposes of this study, the ADL total score was calculated.

The ILS and the ADL were administered in counterbalanced order to a sample of 90 adults from the nonclinical sample (mean = 77 years of age, $SD = 8$) with 30 in each of the Independent, Semi-Independent, and Dependent groups. The time interval between testings ranged from 0 to 42 days (mean = 1, $SD = 5$). The sample consisted of 51% females and 49% males, and 92% Whites, 7% African Americans, and 1% other racial/ethnic origins. Education-level percentages of the sample, as measured by years of schooling, were 31% for 9 years or less, 16% for 10–11 years, 39% for 12–15 years, and 14% for 16 years or more.

Table 5.7 presents the correlations between the two tests. The ADL correlates moderately to moderately high with the ILS, particularly with the ILS Full Scale. While the correlations indicate that the two measures are assessing similar constructs, there is also still enough difference to warrant care in selecting the most appropriate type of instrument. The ILS subscales provide more comprehensive coverage of different areas of functioning than does the ADL, a fact which could account for some of the lack of correspondence. Also, it is expected that a self-report rating could differ from a performance-based score.

Table 5.7. Correlations Between the ILS and the ADL

ILS	ADL	ILS Mean	ILS SD
Subscale			
Memory/Orientation	.67	39.4	14.9
Managing Money	.64	37.7	12.9
Managing Home and Transportation	.60	41.7	14.2
Health and Safety	.65	41.0	14.8
Social Adjustment	.53	44.5	12.0
Factor			
Problem Solving	.61	38.7	13.9
Performance/Information	.66	40.8	13.5
Full Scale	.71	83.1	20.7
ADL			
Mean	41.1		
SD	8.9		

Criterion-Related Validity: Establishing Cut Scores

There was no existing assessment of functional competence to serve as a "gold standard" to establish the sensitivity (in this case, correct classification of adults living dependently) and the specificity (correct classification of adults living independently) for criterion-referenced cut scores for the ILS. Rather, living status (see Chapter 2) provided the validation of the cut scores. In order to derive the cut scores, the distribution of scores for the Independent group and for the Dependent group was utilized. Cut scores were set for each of the subscales, the factors, and the Full Scale.

Three cut scores were decided upon. Two cut scores were chosen to provide the highest sensitivity with a moderate level of specificity, or vice versa. For example, the highest cut score would capture the largest percentage of the nonclinical Dependent adults scoring below the cut score with a moderate percentage of nonclinical Independent adults scoring at or above that cut score. The lowest cut score would identify the largest percentage of Independent adults scoring at or above the cut score while still identifying a moderate percentage of Dependent adults scoring below the cut score. These two cut scores delimit the three classifications: high functioning, moderate functioning, and low functioning. The third cut score represents the score at which sensitivity and specificity are the highest and the most comparable. This cut score occurs within the moderate-functioning range.

Table 5.8 contains the cut scores and the percentages in the Independent and Dependent nonclinical groups that are considered correctly identified by the cut score according to subscale, factor, and Full Scale. The highest cut score identifies a greater percentage of the adults (76%–91%) in the Dependent group as moderate and low functioning (sensitivity), whereas 59% to 70% of adults in the Independent group are classified in the high-functioning range (specificity). The opposite occurs for the lowest cut score; a high percentage of adults (86%–90%) in the Independent group are identified as moderate to high functioning, and 55%–73% of adults who were in the Dependent group were considered to be low functioning. According to the middle cut score, the percentage of Dependent adults scoring below the cut score ranges from 62% to 81%, depending upon subscale, factor, or Full Scale. The percentage of Independent adults scoring at or above the cut score ranges from 76% to 81%.

Table 5.9 shows the percentages of each living status (Independent, Semi-Independent, Dependent) within each level of ILS functioning (high, moderate, low). The Semi-Independent group included adults who needed assistance with some activities of daily living, though the assistance was limited. This table reveals that, for any one area of ability, roughly a third of the Semi-Independent group is classified in each of the three levels of functioning. Because living status is based upon one score, because it is based upon functioning in areas that are less comprehensive than those of the ILS, and because it is based upon a self-report instrument, the correspondence with the ILS levels of functioning is less than perfect.

Table 5.10 demonstrates that the Semi-Independent group falls between the Dependent and Independent groups in terms of the percentages scoring above the middle cut score on any combination of one to five subscales. A greater percentage of the Independent group scored above the middle cut score on one or more subscales than did either the Semi-Independent or Dependent groups. The Dependent group had the smallest percent scoring above the middle cut score.

Construct Validity: Studies With Clinical Populations

For the ILS to be a more clinically useful instrument, validity was established with individuals with diagnoses that involve cognitive impairment. Data were collected on adults with mental retardation, traumatic brain injury, dementia, or a chronic psychiatric disturbance. These groups of adults were expected to have lower functional abilities, at least in some areas, than would a nonclinical sample of adults who were living independently.

Table 5.8. Percentages Classified With the Cut Scores for the Dependent and Independent Groups

	Cut Score	Dependent Group[a]	Independent Group[b]
Subscale			
Memory/Orientation	50	84	59
	45	**73**	**76**
	40	64	87
Managing Money	50	81	65
	45	**75**	**78**
	40	69	86
Managing Home and Transportation	50	78	70
	45	**71**	**81**
	40	59	90
Health and Safety	50	84	65
	45	**73**	**80**
	40	69	86
Social Adjustment	50	76	58
	45	**62**	**78**
	40	55	87
Factor			
Problem Solving	50	79	68
	45	**78**	**78**
	40	67	89
Performance/Information	50	83	63
	45	**74**	**79**
	40	59	90
Full Scale	100	91	62
	92	**81**	**80**
	85	73	89

Note. The bold numbers in the cut score column are the cut scores at which the percentages of Dependent adults with scores below the cut score and Independent adults with scores at or above the cut score is most comparable. The bold numbers in the Dependent Group and Independent Group columns are the corresponding percentages for that group.

[a]Percent of adults in the Dependent group with scores below the cut score.

[b]Percent of adults in the Independent group with scores at or above the cut score.

Three types of analyses were performed to compare each of the clinical groups with a control group, matched for sex and education level, from the Independent nonclinical group. (In the tables, each matched control group is numbered to distinguish one from another.) It was not possible to match for age because the clinical groups included younger adults between the ages of 17 and 64. There was a significant difference in age between the clinical groups and their matched control groups, except for the group of adults with dementia. First, a chi-square statistic was computed to test the interdependency between two factors: level of functioning according to ILS cut scores (high functioning, moderate functioning, and low functioning) and clinical status (e.g., adults with mental retardation versus a nonclinical Independent, matched control group). The chi-square indicates whether the clinical group, in comparison to the

Table 5.9. Percentages Scoring in Each ILS Level of Functioning by Living Status

| | Level of Functioning[a] | Living Status | | |
		Dependent	Semi-Independent	Independent
Subscale				
Memory/ Orientation	Low	64	32	13
	Moderate	20	34	28
	High	16	34	59
Managing Money	Low	69	35	14
	Moderate	12	31	21
	High	19	34	65
Managing Home and Transportation	Low	59	30	9
	Moderate	19	27	21
	High	22	43	70
Health and Safety	Low	69	39	14
	Moderate	15	16	21
	High	16	45	65
Social Adjustment	Low	55	29	13
	Moderate	21	25	29
	High	24	46	58
Factor				
Problem Solving	Low	68	35	11
	Moderate	11	18	21
	High	21	47	68
Performance/ Information	Low	59	32	10
	Moderate	24	31	27
	High	17	37	63
Full Scale	Low	73	38	11
	Moderate	18	29	27
	High	9	33	62

[a]Low = score less than 40 (85 for the Full Scale); Moderate = score between 40 and 49 (85 and 99 for the Full Scale); High = score greater than or equal to 50 (100 for the Full Scale).

nonclinical group, has a different distribution across level of functioning. Second, mean differences between the clinical group and the matched control group were also tested for each subscale, both factors, and the Full Scale. A MANOVA was first conducted to test for an overall effect due to clinical status (using Wilks's Λ), followed by univariate ANOVAs for each subscale, both factors, and the Full Scale. (Paired t tests were not considered necessary as R^2 was less than .10 when the ILS score was regressed onto sex and education level.) The means are included to test the differences in the scores as continuous, rather than categorical variables. Third, the percentage of each clinical and matched control group classified according to all three ILS cut scores is presented to assist in selection of a cut score when the ILS is used with a similar clinical population.

Table 5.10. Percentages Scoring Above the Middle Cut Score on Subscales by Living Status

Number of Subscales	Living Status		
	Dependent	Semi-Independent	Independent
1 Subscale	63.3	88.0	98.0
2 Subscales	36.7	75.0	91.8
3 Subscales	30.0	62.0	85.3
4 Subscales	15.6	42.0	75.0
5 Subscales	4.4	25.0	46.5

Adults With Mental Retardation

The ILS was administered to 70 adults ages 18 to 69 (mean = 34 years, $SD = 12$) who had WAIS–R Full Scale IQ scores ranging from 52 to 84. The group consisted of 43% females and 57% males, and 66% Whites, 28% Hispanics, and 6% African Americans. Education-level percentages of the group, as measured in years of schooling, were 16% for 9 years or less, 14% for 10–11 years, 69% for 12–15 years, and 1% unknown. Marital-status percentages of the group were 96% single, 1% married, and 3% divorced. Fifty had WAIS–R Full Scale IQ scores ranging from 52 to 69 (mild mental retardation) and 20 had WAIS–R Full Scale IQ scores ranging from 71 to 84 (borderline intellectual functioning) as categorized in the *Diagnostic and Statistical Manual of Mental Disorders—Fourth Edition* (DSM–IV; American Psychiatric Association, 1994).

Table 5.11 presents results from a chi-square analysis. For adults with mild mental retardation, all five subscales, both factors, and the Full Scale show an interdependency between the adult's level of functioning and clinical status. There also exists an interdependency among level of functioning and clinical status for the adults with borderline intellectual functioning, except for two subscales: Memory/Orientation and Social Adjustment. Similarly, the means between the adults with mild mental retardation and the Independent group were significantly different for all subscales, both factors, and the Full Scale. Also, the means between the adults with borderline intellectual functioning and the Independent group were significantly different except for Memory/Orientation and Social Adjustment (see Table 5.12). Additionally, there is a significant difference between the means for the adults with mild mental retardation and for the adults with borderline intellectual functioning on all subscales (except Social Adjustment), both factors and the Full Scale, as shown in Table 5.13. Table 5.14 provides the percentages who have scores below each cut score. As with the results from the chi-square analysis and ANOVAs, the lower percentages of adults with mild mental retardation or borderline intellectual functioning who fall below the cut scores indicate that this population of adults performs better on the Memory/Orientation and Social Adjustment subscales than on the other ILS subscales.

Table 5.11. Adults With Mental Retardation: Percentages by ILS Classification in Comparison to Independent Matched Control Groups

		Level of Functioning		
	Group[a]	High	Moderate	Low
Mild MR				
Subscale				
Memory/ Orientation**	Independent 1	66	22	12
	Mild MR	16	26	58
Managing Money**	Independent 1	66	16	18
	Mild MR	0	0	100
Managing Home and Transportation**	Independent 1	64	28	8
	Mild MR	0	4	96
Health and Safety**	Independent 1	72	18	10
	Mild MR	0	0	100
Social Adjustment**	Independent 1	30	46	24
	Mild MR	16	22	62
Factor				
Problem Solving**	Independent 1	68	22	10
	Mild MR	0	0	100
Performance/ Information**	Independent 1	48	34	18
	Mild MR	0	0	100
Full Scale**	Independent 1	58	26	16
	Mild MR	0	0	100
Borderline IQ				
Subscale				
Memory/ Orientation	Independent 2	50	35	15
	Borderline IQ	45	45	10
Managing Money**	Independent 2	60	20	20
	Borderline IQ	5	25	70
Managing Home and Transportation**	Independent 2	65	25	10
	Borderline IQ	20	35	45
Health and Safety**	Independent 2	75	15	10
	Borderline IQ	20	25	55
Social Adjustment	Independent 2	20	35	45
	Borderline IQ	10	60	30
Factor				
Problem Solving**	Independent 2	65	20	15
	Borderline IQ	10	35	55
Performance/ Information**	Independent 2	40	40	20
	Borderline IQ	5	35	60
Full Scale**	Independent 2	45	35	20
	Borderline IQ	5	45	50

[a]Independent 1, $n = 50$; Mild MR, $n = 50$; Independent 2, $n = 20$; Borderline IQ, $n = 20$.

*Chi-square significant at the .05 level.

**Chi-square significant at the .01 level.

Adults with ...	
Mental Retardation	**MR**
Mild Mental Retardation	**Mild MR**
Borderline Intellectual Functioning	**Borderline IQ**

Table 5.12. Adults With Mental Retardation: Means and Standard Deviations in Comparison to Independent Matched Control Groups

	Group[a]	Mean	SD
Mild MR[b]			
Subscale			
Memory/Orientation**	Independent 1	50.5	9.4
	Mild MR	37.1	12.8
Managing Money**	Independent 1	50.2	9.6
	Mild MR	20.2	1.0
Managing Home and Transportation**	Independent 1	50.2	6.5
	Mild MR	23.6	6.2
Health and Safety**	Independent 1	51.9	7.9
	Mild MR	22.3	4.9
Social Adjustment**	Independent 1	45.6	9.1
	Mild MR	36.0	12.3
Factor			
Problem Solving**	Independent 1	50.9	8.4
	Mild MR	20.7	2.4
Performance/Information**	Independent 1	47.8	8.2
	Mild MR	23.6	5.3
Full Scale**	Independent 1	98.5	13.3
	Mild MR	57.2	5.8
Borderline IQ[c]			
Subscale			
Memory/Orientation	Independent 2	48.6	10.7
	Borderline IQ	48.8	10.2
Managing Money**	Independent 2	49.3	10.5
	Borderline IQ	32.4	11.0
Managing Home and Transportation**	Independent 2	49.8	6.4
	Borderline IQ	39.1	11.7
Health and Safety**	Independent 2	52.9	8.5
	Borderline IQ	36.5	13.2
Social Adjustment	Independent 2	42.5	9.7
	Borderline IQ	41.3	10.7
Factor			
Problem Solving**	Independent 2	50.6	9.7
	Borderline IQ	34.2	13.2
Performance/Information*	Independent 2	46.3	10.1
	Borderline IQ	38.6	8.9
Full Scale**	Independent 2	95.0	16.2
	Borderline IQ	78.4	17.8

[a]Independent 1, $n = 50$; Mild MR, $n = 50$; Independent 2, $n = 20$; Borderline IQ, $n = 20$.

[b]For the Independent 1 and Mild MR groups, MANOVA: $F = 80.65$; $p < .001$.

[c]For the Independent 2 and Borderline IQ groups, MANOVA: $F = 4.95$; $p < .001$.

*ANOVA significant at the .05 level.

**ANOVA significant at the .01 level.

Adults with ...	
Mental Retardation	**MR**
Mild Mental Retardation	**Mild MR**
Borderline Intellectual Functioning	**Borderline IQ**

Table 5.13. Adults With Mental Retardation: Means and Standard Deviations for the Mild Mental Retardation Group and the Borderline Intellectual Functioning Group

	Group[a]	Mean	SD
Subscale			
Memory/Orientation**	Mild MR	37.5	12.8
	Borderline IQ	48.8	10.2
Managing Money**	Mild MR	20.2	1.0
	Borderline IQ	32.4	11.0
Managing Home and Transportation**	Mild MR	23.7	6.2
	Borderline IQ	39.1	11.7
Health and Safety**	Mild MR	22.6	5.1
	Borderline IQ	36.5	13.2
Social Adjustment	Mild MR	36.4	12.2
	Borderline IQ	41.3	10.7
Factor			
Problem Solving**	Mild MR	20.8	2.4
	Borderline IQ	34.2	13.2
Performance/Information**	Mild MR	24.1	5.9
	Borderline IQ	39.5	9.0
Full Scale**	Mild MR	57.4	6.0
	Borderline IQ	78.4	17.8

Note. MANOVA: $F = 9.54$; $p < .001$.

[a]Mild MR, $n = 50$; Borderline IQ, $n = 20$.

**ANOVA significant at the .01 level.

Adults with ...	
Mental Retardation	**MR**
Mild Mental Retardation	**Mild MR**
Borderline Intellectual Functioning	**Borderline IQ**

Table 5.14. Adults With Mental Retardation: Percentages Scoring Below the Cut Scores

	Cut Score	Mild MR[a]	Borderline IQ[b]
Subscale			
Memory/Orientation	50	84	55
	45	62	25
	40	56	10
Managing Money	50	100	95
	45	100	85
	40	100	70
Managing Home and Transportation	50	100	80
	45	100	60
	40	96	45
Health and Safety	50	100	80
	45	100	55
	40	100	55
Social Adjustment	50	84	90
	45	74	55
	40	60	30
Factor			
Problem Solving	50	100	90
	45	100	70
	40	100	55
Performance/Information	50	100	95
	45	100	70
	40	100	35
Full Scale	100	100	95
	92	100	70
	85	100	50

[a] $n = 50$.
[b] $n = 20$.

Adults with ...	
Mental Retardation	**MR**
Mild Mental Retardation	**Mild MR**
Borderline Intellectual Functioning	**Borderline IQ**

Adults With Traumatic Brain Injury

The ILS was administered to 48 adults, ages 17 to 78 (mean = 36 years, SD = 16), who had experienced a traumatic brain injury where level of consciousness was altered and/or evidence of neurologic damage was evident. The percentages of adults in the group, according to Bigler's (1988) severity of injury classification scheme, were 25% mild, 23% moderate, 44% severe, and 8% profound. Ten percent of the group had an open head injury, and 90% of the group had a closed head injury. The group consisted of 42% females and 58% males, and 79% Whites, 8% African Americans, 6% Hispanics, 2% Native Americans, and 4% other racial/ethnic origins. Education-level percentages of the group, as measured in years of schooling, were 4% for 9 years or less, 21% for 10–11 years, 69% for 12–15 years, and 6% for 16 years or more. Marital-status percentages of the group were 60% single, 23% married, 13% divorced, and 4% widowed.

Two groups of adults were formed according to severity of injury: one comprised of the adults with mild or moderate traumatic brain injury (n = 23) and the other comprised of the adults with severe or profound traumatic brain injury (n = 25). According to the chi-squares, adults with severe or profound brain injury had a lower level of functioning than did the nonclinical, Independent group in terms of Managing Money, Health and Safety, Problem Solving, and the Full Scale (see Table 5.15). There were no significant differences between the adults with mild or moderate brain injury and the Independent group. The means in Table 5.16 replicate this finding for the adults with severe or profound brain injury. The means for the adults with mild or moderate brain injury have to be interpreted with some caution. The MANOVA showed only a trend for the difference between this group and the control group (p < .10). The ANOVAs suggest that the adults with mild or moderate brain injury perform more poorly on Managing Money, Health and Safety, and Problem Solving than do the adults in the nonclinical control group. Table 5.17 presents the percentages scoring below the three ILS cut scores. A greater percentage of the adults with mild or moderate brain injury scored as moderate to low functioning on the Social Adjustment subscale than on any other subscale or factor. The largest percentage of the adults with severe or profound brain injury scored in the moderate- to low-functioning range on the Managing Money and Health and Safety subscales and on the Problem-Solving factor.

Table 5.15. Adults With Traumatic Brain Injury: Percentages by ILS Classification in Comparison to Independent Matched Control Groups

		Level of Functioning		
	Group[a]	High	Moderate	Low
Mild/Moderate				
Subscale				
Memory/	Independent 3	61	30	9
Orientation	Mild/Moderate	61	22	17
Managing	Independent 3	70	13	17
Money	Mild/Moderate	39	30	31
Managing Home	Independent 3	74	13	13
and Transportation	Mild/Moderate	74	9	17
Health and	Independent 3	74	13	13
Safety	Mild/Moderate	52	17	31
Social	Independent 3	26	35	39
Adjustment	Mild/Moderate	26	22	52
Factor				
Problem	Independent 3	70	13	17
Solving	Mild/Moderate	39	30	31
Performance/	Independent 3	52	35	13
Information	Mild/Moderate	48	39	13
Full Scale	Independent 3	57	26	17
	Mild/Moderate	30	39	31
Severe/Profound				
Subscale				
Memory/	Independent 4	60	28	12
Orientation	Severe/Profound	52	24	24
Managing	Independent 4	64	16	20
Money**	Severe/Profound	4	40	56
Managing Home	Independent 4	68	20	12
and Transportation	Severe/Profound	64	20	16
Health and	Independent 4	76	12	12
Safety**	Severe/Profound	12	32	56
Social	Independent 4	28	32	40
Adjustment	Severe/Profound	32	28	40
Factor				
Problem	Independent 4	68	16	16
Solving**	Severe/Profound	4	32	64
Performance/	Independent 4	48	36	16
Information	Severe/Profound	24	52	24
Full Scale*	Independent 4	52	28	20
	Severe/Profound	16	40	44

[a]Independent 3, $n = 23$; Mild/Moderate, $n = 23$; Independent 4, $n = 25$; Severe/Profound, $n = 25$.

*Chi-square significant at the .05 level.

**Chi-square significant at the .01 level.

Adults with ...	
Traumatic Brain Injury	**TBI**
Traumatic Brain Injury of Mild or Moderate Severity	**Mild/Moderate**
Traumatic Brain Injury of Severe or Profound Severity	**Severe/Profound**

Table 5.16. Adults With Traumatic Brain Injury: Means and Standard Deviations in Comparison to Independent Matched Control Groups

	Group[a]	Mean	*SD*
Mild/Moderate[b]			
Subscale			
Memory/Orientation	Independent 3	50.5	10.0
	Mild/Moderate	49.6	12.4
Managing Money*	Independent 3	50.7	10.9
	Mild/Moderate	43.2	11.4
Managing Home and Transportation	Independent 3	50.8	7.1
	Mild/Moderate	49.3	10.9
Health and Safety**	Independent 3	53.8	9.1
	Mild/Moderate	44.7	12.9
Social Adjustment	Independent 3	43.7	9.1
	Mild/Moderate	39.0	12.8
Factor			
Problem Solving*	Independent 3	51.4	11.0
	Mild/Moderate	42.5	11.9
Performance/Information	Independent 3	47.9	10.0
	Mild/Moderate	47.0	10.3
Full Scale	Independent 3	97.8	16.8
	Mild/Moderate	90.3	17.2
Severe/Profound[c]			
Subscale			
Memory/Orientation	Independent 4	50.1	10.0
	Severe/Profound	46.9	12.7
Managing Money**	Independent 4	50.1	10.9
	Severe/Profound	36.0	9.9
Managing Home and Transportation	Independent 4	50.5	6.8
	Severe/Profound	48.4	8.0
Health and Safety**	Independent 4	53.2	8.7
	Severe/Profound	36.7	10.9
Social Adjustment	Independent 4	43.8	9.5
	Severe/Profound	42.2	12.4
Factor			
Problem Solving**	Independent 4	51.1	10.6
	Severe/Profound	35.0	10.4
Performance/Information	Independent 4	47.6	9.7
	Severe/Profound	43.1	9.3
Full Scale	Independent 4	97.3	16.5
	Severe/Profound	83.7	15.7

[a]Independent 3, $n = 23$; Mild/Moderate, $n = 23$; Independent 4, $n = 25$; Severe/Profound, $n = 25$.

[b]For the Independent 3 and Mild/Moderate groups, MANOVA: $F = 2.09$; $p < .10$.

[c]For the Independent 4 and Severe/Profound groups, MANOVA: $F = 7.29$; $p < .001$.

*ANOVA significant at the .05 level.

**ANOVA significant at the .01 level.

Adults with ...	
Traumatic Brain Injury	**TBI**
Traumatic Brain Injury of Mild or Moderate Severity	**Mild/Moderate**
Traumatic Brain Injury of Severe or Profound Severity	**Severe/Profound**

Table 5.17. Adults With Traumatic Brain Injury: Percentages Scoring Below the Cut Scores

	Cut Score	Mild/ Moderate[a]	Severe/ Profound[b]
Subscale			
Memory/Orientation	50	39	46
	45	26	25
	40	17	21
Managing Money	50	61	96
	45	35	76
	40	30	56
Managing Home and Transportation	50	26	36
	45	22	20
	40	17	16
Health and Safety	50	48	88
	45	35	68
	40	30	56
Social Adjustment	50	74	68
	45	74	40
	40	52	40
Factor			
Problem Solving	50	61	96
	45	52	76
	40	30	64
Performance/Information	50	52	75
	45	26	46
	40	13	17
Full Scale	100	70	83
	92	44	58
	85	30	42

[a]$n = 23$.
[b]$n = 25$.

Adults with ...	
Traumatic Brain Injury	**TBI**
Traumatic Brain Injury of Mild or Moderate Severity	**Mild/Moderate**
Traumatic Brain Injury of Severe or Profound Severity	**Severe/Profound**

Adults With Dementia

The ILS was administered to 20 adults, ages 66 to 88 (mean = 78 years, $SD = 6$), who were diagnosed with dementia (nonspecified), Parkinson's disease, or Huntington's disease. The group consisted of 45% females and 55% males, and 90% Whites and 10% African Americans. Education-level percentages of the group, as measured by years of schooling, were 25% for 9 years or less, 25% for 10–11 years, 40% for 12–15 years, and 10% for 16 years or more. Marital-status percentages of the group were 40% married, 5% divorced, and 55% widowed.

The chi-square statistic was significant for Managing Money and Problem Solving. The percentages in Table 5.18 indicate that more adults with dementia had scores in the moderate- or low-functioning range than did the adults in the nonclinical matched control group for this subscale and factor. The MANOVA did not show a significant difference between the two groups, possibly because the sample size was small. Mean differences were significant for all subscales (except Memory/Orientation and Social Adjustment), both factors, and the Full Scale, according to the separate ANOVAs (see Table 5.19); however, the results from the ANOVAs must be interpreted with caution because the MANOVA was not significant. The percentages classified according to the cut scores are presented in Table 5.20. All of the subscales except Health and Safety classify a large percentage of the adults with dementia as moderate functioning when the highest cut score is used. Managing Money, Social Adjustment, and Performance/Information classify the largest percentage as low functioning when the middle cut score is used.

Table 5.18. Adults With Dementia: Percentages by ILS Classification in Comparison to an Independent Matched Control Group

	Group	Level of Functioning		
		High	**Moderate**	**Low**
Subscale				
Memory/ Orientation	Independent 5	65	10	25
	Dementia	30	30	40
Managing Money*	Independent 5	60	10	30
	Dementia	15	30	55
Managing Home and Transportation	Independent 5	55	25	20
	Dementia	30	35	35
Health and Safety	Independent 5	55	25	20
	Dementia	40	15	45
Social Adjustment	Independent 5	25	45	30
	Dementia	20	35	45
Factor				
Problem Solving*	Independent 5	55	25	20
	Dementia	20	25	55
Performance/ Information	Independent 5	45	30	25
	Dementia	15	35	50
Full Scale	Independent 5	35	35	30
	Dementia	15	20	65

Note. For each group, $n = 20$.

*Chi-square significant at the .05 level.

Table 5.19. Adults With Dementia: Means and Standard Deviations in Comparison to an Independent Matched Control Group

	Group	Mean	SD
Subscale			
Memory/Orientation	Independent 5	48.6	12.5
	Dementia	41.3	14.7
Managing Money**	Independent 5	48.3	11.9
	Dementia	34.9	12.6
Managing Home and Transportation*	Independent 5	48.6	8.4
	Dementia	41.0	11.4
Health and Safety*	Independent 5	49.9	9.3
	Dementia	40.6	13.9
Social Adjustment	Independent 5	44.3	8.2
	Dementia	39.5	11.3
Factor			
Problem Solving**	Independent 5	48.2	11.2
	Dementia	36.2	12.8
Performance/Information*	Independent 5	45.9	10.6
	Dementia	37.4	11.3
Full Scale*	Independent 5	93.7	17.3
	Dementia	78.9	18.3

Note. For each group, $n = 20$; MANOVA: $F = 1.63$; $p < .20$.

*ANOVA significant at the .05 level.

**ANOVA significant at the .01 level.

Table 5.20. Adults With Dementia: Percentages Scoring Below the Cut Scores

	Cut Score	Dementia
Subscale		
Memory/Orientation	50	70
	45	45
	40	40
Managing Money	50	84
	45	74
	40	53
Managing Home and Transportation	50	70
	45	60
	40	35
Health and Safety	50	60
	45	45
	40	45
Social Adjustment	50	80
	45	70
	40	45
Factor		
Problem Solving	50	79
	45	68
	40	53
Performance/Information	50	85
	45	75
	40	45
Full Scale	100	84
	92	63
	85	58

Note. $N = 20$.

Adults With Chronic Psychiatric Disturbance

The ILS was administered to 110 adults, ages 18 to 84 (mean = 51 years, $SD = 16$), who were diagnosed with a chronic psychiatric disturbance. (Two adults with chronic psychiatric disturbance could not be matched with an adult from the control group.) Diagnoses included Major Depression (47%), Schizophrenia (23%), and other (30%—Bipolar Disorder, Generalized Anxiety Disorder, Dysthymic Disorder, Personality Disorder, Alcohol Dependence, and Schizoaffective Disorder). Thirty percent of the group had a psychotic disorder, 66% had a mood disorder, 1% had an anxiety disorder, and 3% had a disorder of another type. Percentages for the lowest reported rating on the Global Assessment of Functioning (GAF) from the DSM–IV were 25% for 25–40, 35% for 45–55, and 40% for 60–80. The group consisted of 55% females and 45% males, and 58% Whites, 29% African Americans, 10% Hispanics, and 3% other racial/ethnic origins. Education-level percentages of the group, as measured by years of schooling, were 11% for 9 years or less, 14% for 10–11 years, 64% for 12–15 years, 9% for 16 years or more, and 2% for unknown. Marital-status percentages of the group were 40% single, 22% married, 26% divorced, and 12% widowed.

For the adults with chronic psychiatric disturbance, the chi-square was significant for all of the subscales, both factors, and the Full Scale (see Table 5.21). This group of adults was divided into three groups according to the GAF. Significantly more adults with a GAF of 25–40 fell in the lowest level of functioning with respect to Managing Money, Health and Safety, Social Adjustment, Problem Solving, Performance/Information, and the Full Scale. For adults with a GAF of 45–55, clinical status and level of functioning were interdependent for Managing Money, Health and Safety, Problem Solving, Performance/Information, and the Full Scale. Adults with a GAF of 60–80 had larger percentages in the moderate- or low-functioning range for Managing Money, Problem Solving, and the Full Scale.

Mean differences were significant for the Full Scale, both factors, and all the subscales (except Memory/Orientation) for the entire group of adults with psychiatric disturbance, and for both adults with a low (25–40) or moderate (45–55) GAF (see Table 5.22). There was a significant mean difference between the adults with a high (60–80) GAF and the nonclinical group for Managing Money, Health and Safety, Social Adjustment, Problem Solving, and the Full Scale. The largest percentage of adults with psychiatric disturbance who scored below the high cut score occurs for Managing Money, Social Adjustment, Problem Solving, and the Full Scale (see Table 5.23). In general, the sensitivity of the ILS cut scores is greater for identifying the adults who had the lowest GAF scores. Managing Money and Social Adjustment are the most sensitive subscales across all three levels of GAF.

Table 5.21. Adults With Chronic Psychiatric Disturbance: Percentages by ILS Classification in Comparison to Independent Matched Control Groups

| | Group[a] | Level of Functioning | | |
		High	Moderate	Low
Psychiatric				
Subscale				
Memory/ Orientation*	Independent 6	62	31	7
	Psychiatric	55	26	19
Managing Money**	Independent 6	63	21	16
	Psychiatric	26	30	44
Managing Home and Transportation**	Independent 6	71	22	7
	Psychiatric	59	20	21
Health and Safety**	Independent 6	64	23	13
	Psychiatric	38	25	37
Social Adjustment**	Independent 6	40	43	17
	Psychiatric	20	26	54

[a]Independent 6, $n = 108$; Psychiatric, $n = 108$; Independent 7, $n = 28$; GAF 25–40, $n = 28$; Independent 8, $n = 36$; GAF 45–55, $n = 36$; Independent 9, $n = 44$; GAF 60–80, $n = 44$.

*Chi-square significant at the .05 level.

**Chi-square significant at the .01 level.

Adults with ...	
Chronic Psychiatric Disturbance	**Psychiatric**
Chronic Psychiatric Disturbance Global Assessment of Functioning	
25–40	**GAF 25–40**
45–55	**GAF 45–55**
60–80	**GAF 60–80**

Table 5.21. Adults With Chronic Psychiatric Disturbance: Percentages by ILS Classification in Comparison to Independent Matched Control Groups
(continued)

| | Group[a] | Level of Functioning | | |
		High	Moderate	Low
Factor				
Problem Solving**	Independent 6	60	29	11
	Psychiatric	27	34	39
Performance/ Information*	Independent 6	54	31	15
	Psychiatric	41	29	30
Full Scale**	Independent 6	62	25	13
	Psychiatric	27	30	43
GAF 25–40				
Subscale				
Memory/ Orientation	Independent 7	64	22	14
	GAF 25–40	36	39	25
Managing Money**	Independent 7	64	22	14
	GAF 25–40	14	22	64
Managing Home and Transportation	Independent 7	64	25	11
	GAF 25–40	46	18	36
Health and Safety**	Independent 7	75	14	11
	GAF 25–40	25	14	61
Social Adjustment*	Independent 7	18	46	36
	GAF 25–40	14	14	72
Factor				
Problem Solving**	Independent 7	72	14	14
	GAF 25–40	11	25	64
Performance/ Information*	Independent 7	43	46	11
	GAF 25–40	25	29	46
Full Scale**	Independent 7	54	28	18
	GAF 25–40	14	22	64
GAF 45–55				
Subscale				
Memory/ Orientation	Independent 8	69	17	14
	GAF 45–55	53	22	25
Managing Money**	Independent 8	64	22	14
	GAF 45–55	19	28	53

[a]Independent 6, *n* = 108; Psychiatric, *n* = 108; Independent 7, *n* = 28; GAF 25–40, *n* = 28; Independent 8, *n* = 36; GAF 45–55, *n* = 36; Independent 9, *n* = 44; GAF 60–80, *n* = 44.

*Chi-square significant at the .05 level.

**Chi-square significant at the .01 level.

Adults with ...	
Chronic Psychiatric Disturbance	**Psychiatric**
Chronic Psychiatric Disturbance Global Assessment of Functioning	
25–40	**GAF 25–40**
45–55	**GAF 45–55**
60–80	**GAF 60–80**

Table 5.21. Adults With Chronic Psychiatric Disturbance: Percentages by ILS Classification in Comparison to Independent Matched Control Groups *(continued)*

	Group[a]	Level of Functioning		
		High	Moderate	Low
Managing Home and Transportation	Independent 8	64	25	11
	GAF 45–55	50	22	28
Health and Safety**	Independent 8	72	17	11
	GAF 45–55	33	25	42
Social Adjustment	Independent 8	25	47	28
	GAF 45–55	17	28	55
Factor				
Problem Solving**	Independent 8	72	14	14
	GAF 45–55	22	31	47
Performance/ Information*	Independent 8	44	42	14
	GAF 45–55	33	25	42
Full Scale	Independent 8	55	28	17
	GAF 45–55	22	22	56
GAF 60–80				
Subscale				
Memory/ Orientation	Independent 9	70	25	5
	GAF 60–80	68	21	11
Managing Money*	Independent 9	70	16	14
	GAF 60–80	39	36	25
Managing Home and Transportation	Independent 9	75	18	7
	GAF 60–80	75	18	7
Health and Safety	Independent 9	73	16	11
	GAF 60–80	50	32	18
Social Adjustment	Independent 9	34	41	25
	GAF 60–80	27	32	41
Factor				
Problem Solving*	Independent 9	71	18	11
	GAF 60–80	41	43	16
Performance/ Information	Independent 9	62	27	11
	GAF 60–80	57	32	11
Full Scale*	Independent 9	68	21	11
	GAF 60–80	39	41	20

[a]Independent 6, $n = 108$; Psychiatric, $n = 108$; Independent 7, $n = 28$; GAF 25–40, $n = 28$; Independent 8, $n = 36$; GAF 45–55, $n = 36$; Independent 9, $n = 44$; GAF 60–80, $n = 44$.

*Chi-square significant at the .05 level.

**Chi-square significant at the .01 level.

Adults with ...	
Chronic Psychiatric Disturbance	**Psychiatric**
Chronic Psychiatric Disturbance Global Assessment of Functioning	
25–40	**GAF 25–40**
45–55	**GAF 45–55**
60–80	**GAF 60–80**

Table 5.22. Adults With Chronic Psychiatric Disturbance: Means and Standard Deviations in Comparison to Independent Matched Control Groups

	Group[a]	Mean	SD
Psychiatric[b]			
Subscale			
Memory/Orientation	Independent 6	51.0	8.2
	Psychiatric	48.4	12.1
Managing Money**	Independent 6	50.1	9.3
	Psychiatric	39.5	11.9
Managing Home and	Independent 6	50.6	7.3
Transportation**	Psychiatric	47.2	10.4
Health and Safety**	Independent 6	50.4	8.5
	Psychiatric	43.3	11.5
Social Adjustment**	Independent 6	47.9	8.3
	Psychiatric	38.1	12.6
Factor			
Problem Solving**	Independent 6	49.8	9.0
	Psychiatric	40.1	11.3
Performance/Information**	Independent 6	48.2	7.8
	Psychiatric	43.9	11.1
Full Scale	Independent 6	99.3	13.0
	Psychiatric	85.3	17.8
GAF 25–40[c]			
Subscale			
Memory/Orientation	Independent 7	49.7	10.7
	GAF 25–40	44.5	12.5
Managing Money**	Independent 7	50.4	10.2
	GAF 25–40	33.6	12.5
Managing Home and	Independent 7	50.4	6.7
Transportation**	GAF 25–40	44.2	9.7
Health and Safety**	Independent 7	52.9	8.1
	GAF 25–40	38.7	11.1
Social Adjustment**	Independent 7	43.1	8.9
	GAF 25–40	34.8	12.7
Factor			
Problem Solving**	Independent 7	51.0	9.9
	GAF 25–40	33.9	11.5
Performance/Information**	Independent 7	47.6	9.1
	GAF 25–40	39.4	11.5
Full Scale	Independent 7	97.0	15.0
	GAF 25–40	76.5	18.0

[a]Independent 6, $n = 108$; Psychiatric, $n = 108$; Independent 7, $n = 28$; GAF 25–40, $n = 28$; Independent 8, $n = 36$, GAF 45–55, $n = 36$; Independent 9, $n = 44$; GAF 60–80, $n = 44$.

[b]For the Independent 6 and Psychiatric groups, MANOVA: $F = 13.35$; $p < .001$.

[c]For the Independent 7 and GAF 25–40 groups, MANOVA: $F = 5.85$; $p < .001$.

[d]For the Independent 8 and GAF 45–55 groups, MANOVA: $F = 4.62$; $p < .001$.

[e]For the Independent 9 and GAF 60–80 groups, MANOVA: $F = 4.44$; $p < .001$.

*ANOVA significant at the .05 level.

**ANOVA significant at the .01 level.

Adults with ...	
Chronic Psychiatric Disturbance	**Psychiatric**
Chronic Psychiatric Disturbance Global Assessment of Functioning	
25–40	**GAF 25–40**
45–55	**GAF 45–55**
60–80	**GAF 60–80**

Table 5.22. Adults With Chronic Psychiatric Disturbance: Means and Standard Deviations in Comparison to Independent Matched Control Groups

(continued)

	Group[a]	Mean	SD
GAF 45–55[d]			
Subscale			
Memory/Orientation	Independent 8	50.7	10.4
	GAF 45–55	47.0	13.1
Managing Money**	Independent 8	50.6	10.2
	GAF 45–55	37.2	12.4
Managing Home and Transportation*	Independent 8	49.6	8.2
	GAF 45–55	44.4	12.7
Health and Safety**	Independent 8	51.7	7.5
	GAF 45–55	41.6	13.6
Social Adjustment**	Independent 8	44.9	8.9
	GAF 45–55	36.5	12.8
Factor			
Problem Solving**	Independent 8	50.4	8.9
	GAF 45–55	37.8	12.5
Performance/Information*	Independent 8	47.5	9.6
	GAF 45–55	41.4	12.6
Full Scale**	Independent 8	96.8	15.4
	GAF 45–55	81.4	18.9
GAF 60–80[e]			
Subscale			
Memory/Orientation	Independent 9	52.1	8.0
	GAF 60–80	51.9	10.0
Managing Money**	Independent 9	52.2	9.4
	GAF 60–80	45.2	8.4
Managing Home and Transportation	Independent 9	51.4	6.1
	GAF 60–80	51.4	7.1
Health and Safety**	Independent 9	52.5	7.9
	GAF 60–80	47.8	8.1
Social Adjustment*	Independent 9	46.2	9.1
	GAF 60–80	41.4	11.9
Factor			
Problem Solving**	Independent 9	51.5	9.0
	GAF 60–80	45.8	6.7
Performance/Information	Independent 9	49.4	8.3
	GAF 60–80	48.8	7.3
Full Scale*	Independent 9	100.7	13.5
	GAF 60–80	93.9	12.4

[a]Independent 6, $n = 108$; Psychiatric, $n = 108$; Independent 7, $n = 28$; GAF 25–40, $n = 28$; Independent 8, $n = 36$, GAF 45–55, $n = 36$; Independent 9, $n = 44$; GAF 60–80, $n = 44$.

[b]For the Independent 6 and Psychiatric groups, MANOVA: $F = 13.35$; $p < .001$.

[c]For the Independent 7 and GAF 25–40 groups, MANOVA: $F = 5.85$; $p < .001$.

[d]For the Independent 8 and GAF 45–55 groups, MANOVA: $F = 4.62$; $p < .001$.

[e]For the Independent 9 and GAF 60–80 groups, MANOVA: $F = 4.44$; $p < .001$.

*ANOVA significant at the .05 level.

**ANOVA significant at the .01 level.

Adults with ...	
Chronic Psychiatric Disturbance	**Psychiatric**
Chronic Psychiatric Disturbance Global Assessment of Functioning	
25–40	**GAF 25–40**
45–55	**GAF 45–55**
60–80	**GAF 60–80**

Table 5.23. Adults With Chronic Psychiatric Disturbance: Percentages Scoring Below the Cut Scores

	Cut Score	Psychiatric[a]	GAF 25–40[b]	GAF 45–55[c]	GAF 60–80[d]
Subscale					
Memory/	50	44	63	47	30
Orientation	45	27	41	34	12
	40	19	22	26	9
Managing	50	74	85	82	61
Money	45	59	74	63	45
	40	45	63	55	25
Managing Home	50	41	54	50	25
and Transportation	45	34	46	47	14
	40	22	36	29	7
Health and	50	61	75	65	50
Safety	45	45	68	49	27
	40	37	61	41	18
Social	50	80	86	84	73
Adjustment	45	69	71	74	64
	40	54	71	55	41
Factor					
Problem	50	72	89	76	59
Solving	45	60	78	66	43
	40	39	63	47	16
Performance/	50	59	73	68	43
Information	45	38	54	49	20
	40	28	42	38	11
Full Scale	100	74	88	76	63
	92	55	77	65	33
	85	41	62	51	19

[a]$N = 110$.

[b]$n = 28$.

[c]$n = 38$.

[d]$n = 44$.

Adults with ...	
Chronic Psychiatric Disturbance	**Psychiatric**
Chronic Psychiatric Disturbance Global Assessment of Functioning	
25–40	**GAF 25–40**
45–55	**GAF 45–55**
60–80	**GAF 60–80**

Adults With Major Depression

The ILS was administered to 52 adults, ages 19 to 84 (mean = 53 years, $SD = 15$), who were diagnosed with Major Depression. (One adult with Major Depression could not be matched with an adult from the control group.) The group consisted of 54% females and 46% males, and 54% Whites, 32% African Americans, 10% Hispanics, and 4% other racial/ethnic origins. Percentages for the lowest reported rating on the Global Assessment of Functioning (GAF) from the DSM–IV were: 17% for 25–40, 29% for 45–55, and 54% for 60–80. Education-level percentages of the group, as measured by years of schooling, were 10% for 9 years or less, 13% for 10–11 years, 63% for 12–15 years, 12% for 16 years or more, and 2% for unknown. Marital-status percentages of the group were 27% single, 17% married, 39% divorced, and 17% widowed.

There was a greater percentage of high-functioning Independent adults than high-functioning adults with Major Depression, according to the Managing Money, Health and Safety, and Social Adjustment subscales, the Problem-Solving factor, and the Full Scale (see Table 5.24). Mean differences were also significantly different for these subscales, for the Problem-Solving factor, for the Performance/Information factor, and for the Full Scale (see Table 5.25). In terms of identifying an adult with Major Depression as moderate or low functioning, the Social Adjustment subscale was the most sensitive (see Table 5.26). The number of adults in each level of GAF was too small to analyze separately.

Table 5.24. Adults With Major Depression: Percentages by ILS Classification in Comparison to an Independent Matched Control Group

		Level of Functioning		
	Group	High	Moderate	Low
Subscale				
Memory/	Independent 10	67	23	10
Orientation	Major Depression	63	19	18
Managing	Independent 10	70	20	10
Money**	Major Depression	33	28	39
Managing Home	Independent 10	74	20	6
and Transportation	Major Depression	63	18	19
Health and	Independent 10	76	12	12
Safety**	Major Depression	43	29	28
Social	Independent 10	33	43	24
Adjustment**	Major Depression	18	23	59
Factor				
Problem	Independent 10	71	21	8
Solving**	Major Depression	33	37	30
Performance/	Independent 10	57	33	10
Information	Major Depression	43	31	26
Full Scale	Independent 10	67	21	12
	Major Depression	29	30	41

Note. For each group, *n* = 51.

**Chi-square significant at the .01 level.

Table 5.25. Adults With Major Depression: Means and Standard Deviations in Comparison to an Independent Matched Control Group

	Group	Mean	SD
Subscale			
Memory/Orientation	Independent 10	50.7	9.3
	Major Depression	49.9	11.4
Managing Money**	Independent 10	51.9	8.9
	Major Depression	41.3	11.9
Managing Home and Transportation	Independent 10	51.4	5.7
	Major Depression	48.5	10.3
Health and Safety**	Independent 10	52.8	7.6
	Major Depression	46.0	9.9
Social Adjustment**	Independent 10	46.2	8.5
	Major Depression	36.7	12.0
Factor			
Problem Solving**	Independent 10	51.8	8.3
	Major Depression	42.7	9.9
Performance/Information*	Independent 10	49.2	7.6
	Major Depression	44.9	10.9
Full Scale**	Independent 10	100.3	12.9
	Major Depression	87.2	16.9

Note. For each group, $n = 51$; MANOVA: $F = 7.51$; $p < .001$.

*ANOVA significant at the .05 level.

**ANOVA significant at the .01 level.

Table 5.26. Adults With Major Depression: Percentages Scoring Below the Cut Scores

	Cut Score	Major Depression
Subscale		
Memory/Orientation	50	35
	45	22
	40	16
Managing Money	50	67
	45	54
	40	40
Managing Home and Transportation	50	37
	45	29
	40	19
Health and Safety	50	55
	45	37
	40	25
Social Adjustment	50	83
	45	77
	40	58
Factor		
Problem Solving	50	65
	45	48
	40	29
Performance/Information	50	57
	45	37
	40	24
Full Scale	100	72
	92	46
	85	38

Note. $N = 52$.

Adults With Schizophrenia

The ILS was administered to 25 adults, ages 22 to 80 (mean = 52 years, *SD* = 17), who were diagnosed with Schizophrenia. (One adult with Schizophrenia could not be matched with an adult from the control group.) The group consisted of 56% females and 44% males, and 56% Whites, 20% African Americans, 16% Hispanics, and 8% Asians. Percentages for the lowest reported rating on the Global Assessment of Functioning (GAF) from the DSM–IV were 40% for 25–40, 48% for 45–55, and 12% for 60–80. Education-level percentages of the group, as measured by years of schooling, were 12% for 9 years or less, 24% for 10–11 years, 56% for 12–15 years, 4% for 16 years or more, and 4% unknown. Marital-status percentages of the group were 56% single, 24% married, 12% divorced, and 8% widowed.

Across all analyses (i.e., chi-square, ANOVA, and percentages below the cut scores), the adults with Schizophrenia were found to be lower functioning than the nonclinical group according to the Managing Money and the Health and Safety subscales, the Problem-Solving factor, and the Full Scale (see Tables 5.27 through 5.29). In addition, the Social Adjustment subscale proved to be sensitive to classifying adults with Schizophrenia as moderate to low functioning.

Table 5.27. Adults With Schizophrenia: Percentages by ILS Classification in Comparison to an Independent Matched Control Group

		Level of Functioning		
	Group	**High**	**Moderate**	**Low**
Subscale				
Memory/	Independent 11	50	33	17
Orientation	Schizophrenia	54	21	25
Managing	Independent 11	67	17	16
Money**	Schizophrenia	21	21	58
Managing Home	Independent 11	67	25	8
and Transportation	Schizophrenia	54	21	25
Health and	Independent 11	79	13	8
Safety**	Schizophrenia	21	25	54
Social	Independent 11	17	50	33
Adjustment	Schizophrenia	25	25	50
Factor				
Problem	Independent 11	71	21	8
Solving**	Schizophrenia	12	25	63
Performance/	Independent 11	42	37	21
Information	Schizophrenia	29	33	38
Full Scale**	Independent 11	50	33	17
	Schizophrenia	21	21	58

Note. For each group, *n* = 24.

**Chi-square significant at the .01 level.

Table 5.28. Adults With Schizophrenia: Means and Standard Deviations in Comparison to an Independent Matched Control Group

	Group	Mean	SD
Subscale			
Memory/Orientation	Independent 11	48.2	10.8
	Schizophrenia	46.9	13.8
Managing Money**	Independent 11	50.2	9.9
	Schizophrenia	35.6	12.8
Managing Home and Transportation	Independent 11	50.1	6.3
	Schizophrenia	45.1	11.5
Health and Safety**	Independent 11	53.6	8.2
	Schizophrenia	37.9	12.3
Social Adjustment	Independent 11	43.8	8.2
	Schizophrenia	38.2	14.3
Factor			
Problem Solving**	Independent 11	51.6	8.9
	Schizophrenia	34.0	12.7
Performance/Information	Independent 11	46.6	9.6
	Schizophrenia	41.5	12.3
Full Scale**	Independent 11	96.5	15.2
	Schizophrenia	79.6	20.5

Note. For each group, $n = 24$; MANOVA: $F = 6.70$; $p < .001$.

**ANOVA significant at the .01 level.

Table 5.29. Adults With Schizophrenia: Percentages Scoring Below the Cut Scores

	Cut Score	Schizophrenia
Subscale		
Memory/Orientation	50	48
	45	32
	40	28
Managing Money	50	79
	45	71
	40	58
Managing Home and Transportation	50	48
	45	40
	40	28
Health and Safety	50	80
	45	60
	40	56
Social Adjustment	50	76
	45	72
	40	52
Factor		
Problem Solving	50	88
	45	79
	40	63
Performance/Information	50	71
	45	46
	40	33
Full Scale	100	79
	92	63
	85	58

Note. $N = 25$.

Chapter 6

Interpretation

The ILS was developed to determine areas of strength and weakness in ability to carry out instrumental activities of daily living. The information gathered from the Full Scale, subscales, and factors can be used for designing intervention or for making decisions about the most appropriate custodial arrangements or living environment. The following information is provided as a guide for interpretation and application of the ILS. Two case studies presented at the end of this chapter are illustrations of these principles.

When to Administer the ILS

In general, the ILS should not be administered immediately after a trauma (e.g., stroke) when the individual's cognitive and motor abilities are unstable. The ILS is most appropriately administered when an individual has reached a somewhat stable level of functioning, because then it is possible to determine the type of living arrangements most suitable to the individual's strengths and weaknesses. An assessment may be necessary because of a spouse's death, a stroke, or a traumatic brain injury, as some adults affected by these events may be in the new position of having to depend on others for assistance with daily living activities.

Additionally, the ILS may be used to assess any individuals who have been institutionalized. The ILS can determine whether their level of functioning may have improved (e.g., through intervention) or declined. In terms of a decline, further diagnostic testing may be warranted to determine whether the decline is from progressive cognitive and/or physical deterioration or from being institutionalized. The ILS would also be appropriate for assessing adults who have been temporarily institutionalized for treatment of a diagnosed psychiatric disorder, the purpose being to determine the most independent living environment possible after treatment.

Level of Interpretation

Information can be obtained from the ILS on a variety of levels, ranging from the Full Scale score to the individual item scores. The ILS Full Scale score is a global indicator of whether the adult can live independently (high functioning), semi-independently (moderate functioning), or dependently (low functioning). The subscale scores should then be referred to for more specific information about the adult's level of functioning in a particular area. Information at the item level identifies which aspect of a particular area of daily living is causing the adult's difficulty. For instance, in regard to Managing Home and Transportation, one can determine, by looking at the pattern of responses across the items, whether the individual is having difficulty maintaining the home, utilizing public transportation, or using the telephone. Item-level information is most useful in designing intervention or detailing the type of assistance required. Furthermore, the items that require problem solving are scored in a way that allows a degree of idiosyncrasy in the response. An individual's response may vary depending upon whether the person lives in a rural or urban area, lives alone or with a spouse, or belongs to a particular cohort. In some cases, the individual's response should be investigated to determine whether it is a reasonable response. If the individual's idiosyncratic response is appropriate for his or her circumstances, then this fact should be taken into account by persons interpreting the scores and making recommendations. For example, an individual living in a rural area with no public transportation or telephone service may give responses that are unique but appropriate to such an environment.

The factor scores provide additional information to interpret the individual's performance. In general, the factors contrast reasoning ability (Problem Solving) with the ability to perform simple tasks (Performance/Information). The majority of tasks that make up the Performance/Information factor can be taught (e.g., performing simple mathematical calculations or using a phone). The Problem-Solving factor, however, concerns the individual's ability to apply this knowledge. With respect to Health and Safety, for example, an individual may have factual knowledge about which number to dial in case of an emergency (Performance/Information) but may not comprehend that a doctor should be called if chest pain occurs (Problem Solving).

The screening items facilitate interpretation by providing some basic information about perceptual-motor abilities that could impact performance on the ILS. For example, if an individual has difficulty speaking but is cognitively able to provide a 2-point response to an item (as evidenced through a written response), the clinician should note that an adaptation to the adult's environment is required (e.g., an alert button for the police or medical emergency facility) in order for the adult to act independently in an emergency situation. Another example is the adult who is unable to read, but is otherwise able to function independently; such a person may be able to take some basic reading classes in order to read well enough to understand the directions on medicine bottles or in recipes. An individual who is unable to write but who displays an understanding for managing money may need someone to come to the home once or twice a month to help with writing out bills or other correspondence, rather than someone to serve as a guardian for all financial matters.

Considering the individual's life circumstances is of paramount importance for determining the level of assistance that an individual needs. An older adult, for example, may perform poorly in one area assessed by the ILS because a spouse has always managed that area of life. If the spouse is still able and willing to manage that aspect, changing the living arrangements may be unnecessary despite the examinee's poor performance in this area. On the other hand, the ILS may help objectify an individual's weaknesses so that progress can be made toward helping that person acknowledge and accept some limitations on her or his ability to function independently. The results from the ILS would assist in arranging for the help that is needed while allowing the older adult to maintain as much independence as possible.

In some instances, the individual may be able to live independently (i.e., without the care of others) but may need adaptations made to the environment. For example, an emergency alert system can be installed in the home of an individual with a speech impairment so that police and medical emergency personnel can be notified if the individual is unable to speak adequately over the phone.

Some adults may need limited assistance from others, whether in handling finances, providing care of the household, providing transportation, or preventing social isolation. If an older adult loses a spouse who has managed some activities of everyday living, the older adult may need only some instruction to learn, for example, how to cook meals or how to handle a checkbook. If the older adult's social life has suddenly dwindled, arrangements could be made to have the individual join a senior center. Similarly, an adult who is cognitively impaired, perhaps due to a traumatic brain injury, may need only specific training on how to negotiate certain aspects of life.

Case Studies

Case Study 1

Mary is an 82-year-old African-American female who has 12 years of schooling. She has been a widow for 2 years. She has one daughter who lives in the same city and another who lives out of state. Mary currently lives alone in a house, but her daughters have begun to worry about her ability to take care of herself; they have noticed a decline in her functioning since her husband died. Figure 6.1 depicts her scores as recorded on the ILS Record Form.

According to the screening items, Mary can read the smaller print with the aid of bifocals. The screening items also show that she walks slowly with the aid of a cane.

Mary received full credit for all of the Memory/Orientation items. Her memory does not appear to be a concern; that is, she can remember her phone number and address and recall a list of items and the details of an appointment. She also seems to be well oriented to time and place (she knows the day of the week, her address, and the name of the city).

Her responses to the items on the Managing Money subscale suggest that she understands day-to-day aspects of handling money (writing checks, counting change, knowing why it is important to pay bills). However, she does not appear to understand completely how to manage her money (she exhibited only a partial understanding of what health and home insurance and social security are; she did not know by what date she needed to file her income tax return, how to compute her portion of a payment, or how to protect herself from being cheated out of her money).

According to the Managing Home and Transportation subscale, Mary knows how to use the phone, address an envelope, and utilize public transportation. Someone else monitors the condition of her home; she is unsure about how to get repairs done or how to handle household problems (e.g., if the house is too cold or if the lights were to go out).

In the area of Health and Safety, Mary knows how to call the police, get medical help, and handle her physical care. She does not appear to use the best judgment for ensuring her safety when answering a knock at the door, going out at night, or cutting her hand badly.

In terms of Mary's Social Adjustment, she does not feel good about herself and always feels down. She does not often see or talk to friends.

The scores for Problem Solving and Performance/Information indicate that Mary is usually able to perform basic tasks and has adequate knowledge about various issues, but in a number of instances, she cannot adequately apply information or optimally handle situations that require more complex problem-solving abilities. Her difficulty in demonstrating good judgment concerning her safety or managing her home could place her in danger.

Comments and Recommendations

Mary exhibits enough ability for the present time to remain in her home alone. However, she appears to need certain services. She indicates only peripheral understanding of home maintenance (an area of responsibility previously assumed by her husband); therefore, she would benefit from having someone to perform yard work and other basic repairs. She also needs someone to check on her weekly to monitor the condition of her health as well as her home. Given Mary's negative emotions and limited contact with others, she needs encouragement in improving her social interaction, possibly by participating in activities at a senior citizen center or with a church group. Because of her poor eyesight and mobility, it may be necessary to assess her driving ability and investigate transportation services. With assistance, Mary should be able to remain in her home. If outside support is unavailable or

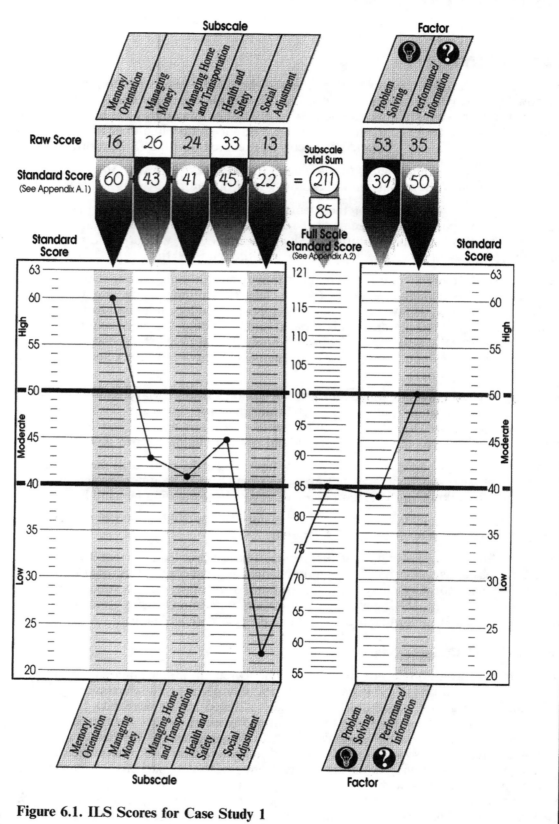

Figure 6.1. ILS Scores for Case Study 1

unsatisfactory, the solution may be to move to a retirement community where she can receive partial services, regular safety checks, and increased social interaction with peers.

Case Study 2

John is a single, 22-year-old White male with 12 years of special education. John's WAIS–R Full Scale IQ was 70 at age 20. He currently lives in a structured setting in a group home. The staff administered the ILS to evaluate John's strengths and weaknesses and to determine whether he is able to move to a less structured living environment. John's scores from the ILS Record Form are shown in Figure 6.2.

John's performance on the Memory/Orientation subscale indicates that he knows his address, telephone number, and the name of the city where he is living. He is also aware of the day of the week and knows how to tell time. However, he has some difficulty with short-term memory (e.g., memorizing a shopping list or remembering a doctor's appointment).

In the area of Managing Money, John knows how he obtains his money, how to count coins, and how to set up a simple math problem; he has a partial understanding of why it is important to pay bills, why he should read a document before signing it, how to avoid being cheated out of his money, and why people make wills. John does not know how to make out a check or money order; he does not have any understanding of health and home insurance; he does not know when income tax is due or how to solve math problems.

With respect to Managing Home and Transportation, John knows how to utilize public transportation and how to use the phone. He has only a partial understanding of how to deal with household problems such as what to do if the lights go out or if the house is too cold.

John's performance on the Health and Safety subscale indicates that he knows how to call the police and get medical help but that he does not fully recognize the potential dangers associated with a fire, gas odor, cutting his hand, or someone knocking on his door at night. John does not recognize the health risks associated with losing 10 pounds quickly or staying in bed all the time.

In terms of Social Adjustment, John feels good about himself and looks forward to tomorrow. He often sees and talks with friends, but he admits that he often gets angry with others.

John exhibits difficulty with situations requiring reasoning ability, as reflected in his score on the Problem-Solving factor. In many areas John cannot perform a given task or does not know the basic information for answering a question (Performance/Information factor). He also has difficulty responding to situations that are new to him. The examiner noted during testing that John needed some items to be rephrased with simpler vocabulary and some items to be phrased more concretely.

Comments and Recommendations

There are many areas of everyday living skills in which John is low functioning, as reflected by the ILS Full Scale score. The factors also indicate that John does not have many of the abilities necessary for independent or semi-independent living. Despite these overall weaknesses, specific items highlight a number of strengths, such as using the phone, counting coins, and remembering his address and telephone number.

Staff members at the group home indicate that John can follow and complete a set of five specific instructions and can cook simple meals. However, they also note that he tends to get stressed and tense when he is presented with a novel situation. Given his pattern of strengths and weaknesses on the ILS and the comments from the staff, John is a good candidate for learning additional specific skills that may equip him to move eventually to a semi-independent setting. Because emergency situations are novel by nature, John's questionable ability to react

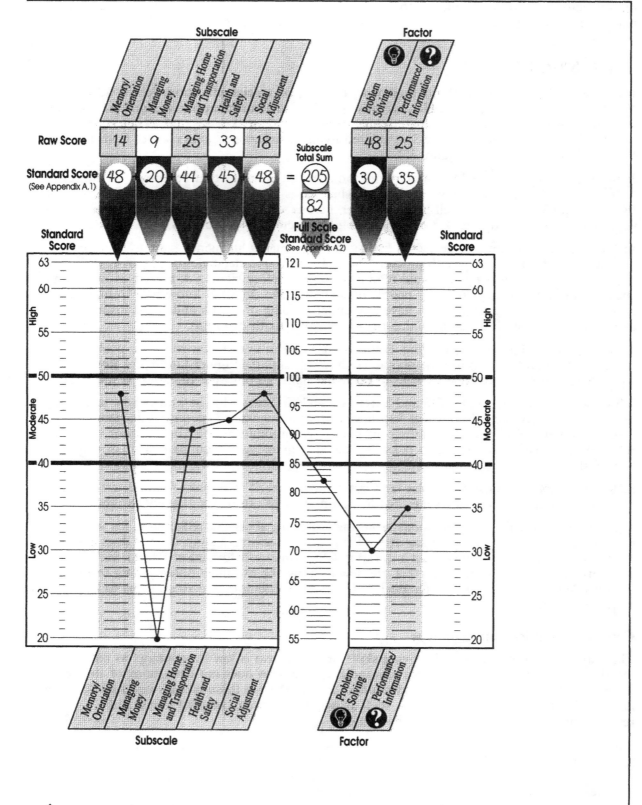

Figure 6.2. ILS Scores for Case Study 2

appropriately and safely in these instances is of some concern. Rehearsing and "overlearning" how to react in specific types of emergencies is recommended for him. John should receive continued supervision and structure, with the degree of supervisory support gradually decreasing as he learns new skills.

As he becomes able to respond with appropriate reactions and to demonstrate the necessary skills, he could move to a less structured environment, such as a supervised apartment. The apartment-living experience would have to be structured to include someone who would be responsible for managing money and taking care of household problems. Such a move will necessarily involve a period of adaptation for easing the novelty of the situation and for troubleshooting problematic or hazardous aspects of the change.

Appendix A

Norms Tables

Table A.1. Subscale and Factor Standard Score Equivalents of Raw Scores

Standard Score	Memory/Orientation	Managing Money	Managing Home and Transportation	Health and Safety	Social Adjustment	Problem Solving	Performance/Information	Standard Score
20	0–9	0–15	0–17	0–24	0–12	0–42	0–15	20
21	–	16	–	–	–	43	16	21
22	–	–	–	–	13	–	–	22
23	–	–	18	25	–	44	17	23
24	–	17	–	–	–	–	18	24
25	10	–	–	–	–	45	–	25
26	–	18	19	26	–	46	19	26
27	–	–	–	–	14	–	20	27
28	–	19	–	27	–	47	–	28
29	–	–	20	–	–	–	21	29
30	–	20	–	–	–	48	–	30
31	11	–	–	28	–	–	22	31
32	–	21	21	–	15	49	23	32
33	–	–	–	–	–	–	–	33
34	–	22	–	29	–	50	24	34
35	–	–	22	–	–	51	25	35
36	12	–	–	30	–	–	–	36
37	–	23	–	–	16	52	26	37
38	–	–	23	–	–	–	27	38
39	–	24	–	31	–	53	–	39
40	–	–	–	–	–	–	28	40
41	–	25	24	–	–	54	29	41
42	13	–	–	32	–	55	–	42
43	–	26	–	–	17	–	30	43
44	–	–	25	–	–	56	31	44
45	–	27	–	33	–	–	–	45
46	–	–	–	–	–	57	32	46
47	–	–	26	34	–	–	33	47
48	14	28	–	–	18	58	–	48
49	–	–	–	–	–	–	34	49
50	–	29	27	35	–	59	35	50
51	–	–	–	–	–	60	–	51
52	–	30	–	–	–	–	36	52
53	–	–	28	36	19	61	37	53
54	15	31	–	–	–	–	–	54
55	–	–	–	37	–	62	38	55
56	–	32	29	–	–	–	39	56
57	–	–	–	–	–	63	–	57
58	–	–	–	38	–	64	40	58
59	–	33	30	–	20	–	41	59
60	16	–		–		65	–	60
61		34		39		–	42	61
62				–		66		62
63				40				63

Table A.2. Full Scale Standard Score Equivalents for the Subscale Total Sum

Full Scale Standard Score	Subscale Total Sum	Full Scale Standard Score	Subscale Total Sum
55	100–138	89	222–223
56	139–140	90	224–226
57	141–143	91	227–228
58	144–145	92	229–231
59	146–148	93	232–233
60	149–150	94	234–236
61	151–153	95	237–238
62	154–155	96	239–241
63	156–158	97	242–243
64	159–160	98	244–246
65	161–163	99	247–248
66	164–165	100	249–251
67	166–168	101	252–253
68	169–170	102	254–256
69	171–173	103	257–258
70	174–175	104	259–261
71	176–178	105	262–263
72	179–180	106	264–266
73	181–183	107	267–268
74	184–185	108	269–271
75	186–188	109	272–273
76	189–190	110	274–276
77	191–193	111	277–278
78	194–195	112	279–281
79	196–198	113	282–283
80	199–200	114	284–286
81	201–203	115	287–288
82	204–205	116	289–291
83	206–208	117	292–293
84	209–210	118	294–296
85	211–213	119	297–298
86	214–215	120	299–301
87	216–218	121	302
88	219–221		

Appendix B

Examiners and Testing Sites

Testing Sites—Nonclinical Sample

Autumn Winds Retirement Lodge, Schertz, TX
Central Recreation Center, San Angelo, TX
Charleston Area Senior Center, Charleston, IL
Charleston Manor, Charleston, IL
Christ The King Episcopal Church,
   Houston, TX
Fairfield Senior Center, Fairfield, CT
Fellowship General Baptist Church,
   Poplar Bluff, MO
First Assembly of God Church Keenagers,
   Pampa, TX
First United Methodist Church, Goldwaite, TX
Jewish Family Services, Dallas, TX
Magee Rehabilitation Hospital,
   Philadelphia, PA
Meadowbrook Manor, Miami, FL
North Cross United Methodist Church,
   Kansas City, MO
Old Town Cruces Association, Las Cruces, NM
Park Home Health, Iowa Park, TX

Psychotherapy Inc., Phoenix, AZ
Romeo-Washington-Bruce Parks & Recreation
   OAC, Romeo, MI
Royal Palace Ballroom, San Antonio, TX
Senior Center, San Angelo, TX
Senior Citizens Services for Jackson Co.,
   Carbondale, IL
Sisters of St. Joseph of Rochester,
   Rochester, NY
St. Dunstan's Adult Daycare Center, Tulsa, OK
St. Francis of Assisi Catholic Church,
   San Antonio, TX
St. Joseph's Manor, Trumbull, CT
St. Luke Cumberland Presbyterian,
   Ft. Worth, TX
Stone Mountain Senior Center,
   Stone Mountain, GA
The Southeastern Wisconsin Center for
   Independent Living, Inc., Milwaukee, WI
Southwest Senior Center, Philadelphia, PA

Examiners by State—Nonclinical Sample

Northeastern Region

Connecticut
Marjy N. Ehmer, PhD
Estelle R. Friedman, PhD
Alberta Gilinsky, PhD
Patricia Shea, MS

Massachusetts
Anthony Paolitto, PhD

New Hampshire
Rita Comtois, PhD
Sarah Warren, PsyD

New Jersey
Verneda Baugh, PhD
Dustin J. Gordon, BA

New York
Kerry Donnelly, PhD
Mina Dunnam, PhD
Phyllis Ladrigan, PhD
Lenore Powell, EdD
Helen W. Schlagel, MS
Annabelle Wolfzahn, PhD

Pennsylvania
Barbara Harris, PhD
Brenda Ivker, PhD

Vermont
Jonathan Rightmyer, PhD

North Central Region

Illinois
William T. Bailey, PhD
Scott Parker, PhD

Indiana
Stana J. Michael, EdD

Iowa
Darcie Randleman, MA

Michigan
Carla L. Barnes, PhD
Gloria Bauer, MA

Missouri
Harold V. Bray, Jr., PhD
Lloyd Kallial, PhD
Toby Lischko, MA

John M. Sebben, BA
Sara Wilcox, MA

Ohio
Joan Speight, PhD
R.L. Stegman, PhD

South Dakota
Kathy Chauncey, MA

Wisconsin
Susan Andrews, PhD
Kenneth Klauck, PhD

Southern Region

Alabama
Martha Jo Daniel, MA
Joyce Elliott, ESD

Florida
David R. Cox, PhD
Cecilia T. Deidan, PhD
Mady Fingeret, PhD
Marshall Jones, PhD

Georgia
Dennis Thompson, PhD

Kentucky
Konnie Torbahn, MA

Oklahoma
Geralann Coldwell, MA

South Carolina
Mary Furchtgott, EdD

Tennessee
Kristen Gilbert, MA

Texas
Donna Anderson, MEd
Mary Beadling, MA, MS
Judy Brumer, MA

Michelle Brummett, EdM
Nancy Drobniak, MA
Cynthia Lindsay, MS
Lynda Newman, PhD
Louise O'Donnell, MA
Cynthia Olson, MS
Fara Raines, MEd
Kim Rausch, MA
Mary Sanders, EdD
Tommy Max Sanders, PhD
Carolyn Segal, PhD
Chris Sidlauskas, MEd
Edith Snider, MA
Jeanne Snyder, MEd
Maggie Stevens, MEd
Donna Wagoner, MEd

Virginia
J.D. Ball, PhD
Mary Vince, MS Ed

Western Region

Arizona
Della Carter, MS
Judith DeGrazia, PhD
Claire Tarte, PhD

California
Kenneth Dellefield, PhD
Larry N. Ferguson, PhD
Valerie Rice, PhD
Sheryl Wilson, PhD

Hawaii
Joan H. Koff, PhD

Montana
Carol Cooley Kraft, MA
Dawn Marie Birk, PhD

New Mexico
John F. Corso, PhD

Washington
Connie Castle, MS
Thomas McKnight, PhD

Examiners and Testing Sites—Clinical Sample

Brockton & West Roxbury VA Medical Center,
Brockton, MA
  Judith S. Aftosmes, RN
  Jennifer Moye, PhD

Goodwill Industries, San Antonio, TX
  Michelle Brummett, EdM
  Haley Gaskell, BA
  Louise O'Donnell, MA
  Kim Rausch, MA

Mission Road Developmental Center,
San Antonio, TX
  Haley Gaskell, BA
  Marcia L. Nichols, BA
  Kristen Wiens, BA

University of Pittsburgh Medical Center,
Brain Trauma Research, Pittsburgh, PA
  Meryl A. Butters, PhD

Southeast Mission Geriatric Services,
San Francisco, CA
  Clare Ames-Klein, PhD
  Joan F. Schwartz, PhD

Fort Lyon VA Medical Center, Fort Lyon, CO
  Madolyne Nancy Bridgewood, MA
  Michael R. Camfield, PsyD

Braintree Rehabilitation Clinic, Fall River, MA
  Janet Bejtlich, MS
  Helaine M. Bilos, BS
  Rhonda L. Jost, BS

Braintree Rehabilitation Clinic,
Framingham, MA
  Janet McBride-Roy, BA

THOMS Rehabilitation Hospital, Asheville, NC
  Mark R. Hill, PhD

Cambridge Speech and Cognitive Rehabilitation
Center, Somerville, MA
  Jennifer A. Carey, BS

Private Practice, Chula Vista, CA
  Kendra A. Allen, MA
  Fred D. Harris, BA
  Sylvia Mende, MA
  Richard E. Townsend, PhD

NSO—Geriatric Screening and Outpatient
Service, Detroit, MI
  John Sczomak, PhD

Naples Neurological Associates, Naples, FL
  David B. Rawlings, PhD

Department of Psychiatry and Behavioral
Sciences, Eastern Virginia Medical School,
Norfolk, VA
  J.D. Ball, PhD

Tangram Rehabilitation Network,
San Marcos, TX
  Melissa Z. Gonzalez, MSSW

Residential Management, Inc.,
San Antonio, TX
  Elaine Dreyer, MA

Transitional Learning Community,
Galveston, TX
  Michelle Brummett, EdM
  Debra Marmor, BA

Private Practice, Houston, TX
  David M. McLendon, PhD

Geriatric Institute, Nova Southeastern
University, Ft. Lauderdale, FL
  William J. Burns, PhD
  Adys Prieto, PsyD
  Leonard Roth, PhD

Dayton Department of VA Medical Center,
Dayton, OH
  R.L. Stegman, PhD

▲ References

American Psychiatric Association. (1994). *Diagnostic and statistical manual of mental disorders* (4th ed.). Washington, DC: Author.

Alexander, G. J., & Lewin, T. H. D. (1972). *The aged and the need for surrogate management.* New York: Syracuse University Press.

Bigler, E. (1988). *Diagnostic clinical neuropsychology* (Rev. ed.). Austin: University of Texas Press.

Committee to Develop Standards for Educational and Psychological Testing. (1985). *Standards for educational and psychological testing.* Washington, DC: American Psychological Association.

Crocker, L., & Algina, J. (1986). *Introduction to classical and modern test theory.* Fort Worth: Holt, Rinehart and Winston.

Dunn, E., Searight, H., Grisso, T., Margolis, R., & Gibbons, J. (1990). The relation of the Halstead-Reitan neuropsychological battery to functional daily living skills in geriatric patients. *Archives of Clinical Neuropsychology, 5,* 103–117.

Grisso, T. (1986). Evaluating competencies: Forensic assessments and instruments. In B. D. Sales (Ed.), *Perspectives in law & psychology* (Vol.7). New York: Plenum.

Grisso, T. (1994). Clinical assessments for legal competence of older adults. In M. Storandt & G. R. VandenBos (Eds.), *Neuropsychological assessment of dementia and depression in older adults: A clinician's guide* (pp. 119–139). Washington, DC: American Psychological Association.

Heaton, R. K., & Pendleton, M. G. (1981). Use of neuropsychological tests to predict adult patients' everyday functioning. *Journal of Consulting and Clinical Psychology, 49,* 807–821.

Horstman, P. M. (1975). Protective services for the elderly: The limits of parens patriae. *Missouri Law Review, 40,* 215–278.

Kaplan, K. H., Strang, J. P., & Ahmed, I. (1988). Dementia, mental retardation, and competency to make decisions. *General Hospital Psychiatry, 10,* 385–388.

Lawton, M.P., & Moss, M. (n.d.). *Philadelphia Geriatric Center Multilevel Assessment Instrument: Manual for full-length MAI.* Philadelphia: Author.

Loeb, P. (1983). "Validity of the Community Competence Scale with the elderly." Unpublished doctoral dissertation, Saint Louis University.

Moye, J. (1996). Theoretical frameworks for competency in cognitively impaired elderly adults. *Journal of Aging Studies, 10* (1), 27–42.

Powell, D. H., Kaplan, E. F., Whitla, D., Weintraub, S., Catlin, R., & Funkenstein, H. H. (1993). *MicroCog: Assessment of cognitive functioning.* San Antonio, TX: The Psychological Corporation.

Ryan, J. J., Paolo, A. M., & Brungardt, T. M. (1990). Standardization of the Wechsler Adult Intelligence Scale–Revised for persons 75 years and older. *Psychological Assessment: A Journal of Consulting and Clinical Psychology, 2,* 404–411.

Sager, M. A., Dunham, N. C., Schwantes, A., Mecum, L., Halverson, K., & Harlowe, D. (1992). Measurement of activities of daily living in hospitalized elderly: A comparison of self-report and performance-based methods. *Journal of the American Geriatrics Society, 40,* 457–462.

Searight, H. (1983). "The utility of the Community Competence Scale for determining placement site among the deinstitutionalized mentally ill." Unpublished doctoral dissertation, Saint Louis University.

Searight, H. R., Dunn, E. J., Grisso, J. T., Margolis, R., & Gibbons, J. L. (1989). Correlation of two competence assessment methods in a geriatric population. *Perceptual and Motor Skills*, 68, 863–872.

Searight, H. R., Oliver, J. M., & Grisso, J. T. (1983). The Community Competence Scale: Preliminary reliability and validity. *American Journal of Community Psychology*, 11, 609–613.

U.S. Bureau of the Census (1993). 1993 Census of Population Housing Authority, Washington, DC: U.S. Bureau of the Census (Producer/Distributor).

Weinberger, M., Samsa, G. P., Schmader, K., Greenberg, S. M., Carr, D. B., & Wildman, D. S. (1992). Comparing proxy and patients' perceptions of patients' functional status: Results from an outpatient geriatric clinic. *Journal of the American Geriatrics Society*, 40, 585–588.

Wechsler, D. (1955). *Wechsler Adult Intelligence Scale.* New York: The Psychological Corporation.

Wechsler, D. (1981). *Wechsler Adult Intelligence Scale—Revised.* San Antonio, TX: The Psychological Corporation.